Demolishing Supposed

BIBLE

Contradictions

VOLUME 2

Exploring Forty Alleged Contradictions

Ken Ham, Bodie Hodge
& Tim Chaffey
EDITORS

First printing: February 2012
Third printing: September 2017

Master Books®, P.O. Box 726, Green Forest, AR 72638
Master Books® is a division of the New Leaf Publishing Group, Inc.

ISBN: 978-0-89051-649-2
ISBN: 978-1-61458-142-0 (digital)
Library of Congress Number: 2010937902

Cover design by Left Coast Design
Cover illustration by Krieg Barrie/World magazine

Unless otherwise noted, Scripture is taken from the New King James
Version of the Bible, copyright © 1982 by Thomas Nelson, Inc. Used
by permission. All rights reserved.

Please consider requesting that a copy of this volume
be purchased by your local library system.

Printed in the United States of America

Please visit our website for other great titles:
www.masterbooks.com

For information regarding author interviews,
please contact the publicity department at (870) 438-5288.

Master
Books®
A Division of New Leaf Publishing Group
www.masterbooks.com

Acknowledgments

We would like to thank the editors and reviewers who graciously gave of their time to help review chapters in this book:

Dr. Terry Mortenson, Ken Ham, Pastor David Chakranarayan, Dr. Tommy Mitchell, Ron Uebel, Tim Chaffey, Bodie Hodge, Frost Smith, Chuck McKnight, Erik Lutz, David Wright, Karin Viet, Roger Patterson, Troy Lacey, Steve Fazekas, and Jeremy Ham.

Contents

Each alleged contradiction could often be listed in multiple places, so we merely selected one of the relevant verses and put it under that section.

Acts–Revelation

A Good Defense Is a Good Offense

← Bodie Hodge and David Wright →

We often hear skeptics attack Christians with pointed questions in an attempt to poke holes in the Christian worldview. In many cases, they directly attack the Bible or the character of God. The debate usually goes something like the following:

1. The skeptic attacks with the first question.
2. The Christian responds to the first question.
3. The skeptic attacks with a second question.
4. The Christian responds to the second question.
5. The skeptic attacks with a third question.
6. The Christian responds to the third question.
7. It continues like this until they part ways.

Many times these debates can be heated, and we've even found numerous instances where the skeptic asks a question and gives no time for a response before he or she fires off another question. Other times, we've seen skeptics ask multiple unrelated questions all at once trying to overwhelm the Christian. But notice the tactic — attack and make the Christian defend his viewpoint until the battle is over. They are trying to make the Christian give up ground with all these attacks.

But in the battle over these humanistic religions and the Bible, should Christians simply be on the defensive? Sooner or later, the Christian needs to have a "Normandy." Normandy was the largest-ever-in-history amphibious offensive to the Nazi invasion of Europe. In other words, the Christian needs to take an offensive in the debate, rather than always staying on the defensive.

Turning the Tide

In fact, we are called to demolish arguments, but unlike the unbeliever (2 Corinthians 10:4–5; Romans 14:6), we need to do this with gentleness, respect, and graciousness (1 Peter 3:15; Colossians 4:6). We can respect a person and be gentle to the person with the same grace the Lord showed to us, while being fierce toward the false philosophy that has taken him or her captive (Ephesians 6:12).

The atheists, agnostics, humanists, and so on are not the enemy — for they are made in the image of God, just as we are, whether they acknowledge it or not. The false ideas of atheism, agnosticism, and humanism are enemies of the truth, and these enemies need to be attacked so the person deceived by them can realize their errors and see the truth. Sadly, many unbelievers do not realize they are merely being used as pawns in a chess match — a spiritual battle between good and evil.

We need to get these unbelievers to realize they have been duped. This is where an attack on their false philosophies becomes important. We need to show them the weakness of their religion. Otherwise, they will continue to think they are standing on a solid foundation, when they aren't. Our battle tactic should change to be as follows:

1. The skeptic attacks with the first question.

2. The Christian responds to the first question[1] and attacks the false philosophy. He should be gentle and respectful to the person but not hold back on the truth or neglect to use Scripture as foundational truth.

---

1. Answers in Genesis has shown on numerous occasions that biblical Christianity is defensible to hostile questions. We've answered the top questions in the creation-evolution and biblical authority debates, and we will continue to do so. Sadly, not all Christians know these answers, but we want to encourage you to have them. A great place to start is with the New Answers Books series (1, 2, and 3) and the general apologetics book series called How Do We Know the Bible Is True? You can also visit us on our website, www.answersingenesis.org.

3. The skeptic defends his philosophy. He will be forced to evaluate his religion to see if it really stands firm. This will be a first for many skeptics.

4. The Christian attacks the false philosophy again.

5. The skeptic defends his philosophy.

6. It continues like this until they part ways. Before this happens, the Christian should look for an opportunity to share the gospel message.

Notice this is not attacking the person but his or her philosophy. You may need to point this out to the person.

Practical Example (Bodie Hodge)

One day I was called to deal with a hostile professing evolutionary atheist who was questioning a young Christian lady. As I approached, the skeptic fired off question after question to the lady and did not even permit her to respond. Every time the Christian tried to respond, the skeptic would ask another question in a rather aggressive tone.

When I cut into the conversation the skeptic turned to me and asked who I was. I kindly told him who I was and gave my credentials. He said something sarcastically to the effect of "finally someone with an education." Then, he launched into a tirade, one question after another attacking Christianity. Every time I tried to respond, he cut me off with another question.

So I changed my tactic. While he took a breath, I slipped in a question that almost silenced him. I asked him, "Why are you wearing clothes?" He was taken back and became speechless. So I asked again and then said something to the effect that "animals don't get up in the morning and put clothes on. You are an atheist, right? You believe people are just animals, so why are you wearing clothes?"

Then he paused and thought for a moment and said, "Because it's cold." So I instantly came back and said, "So when it warms up you don't wear clothes?" He was speechless. Obviously, he had not considered, in his professed worldview, why he wore clothes. Yet there he was with shirt and pants on. (Thankfully!)

I explained that he "wears clothes because in a literal Genesis, a literal Adam and a literal Eve ate a literal fruit and literally disobeyed God, and that caused us to be literally shameful. So we wear clothes as a result. And in your heart of hearts, you know God exists, and your actions reveal that you know you are shameful (Romans 1)."

Then I noticed he was wearing a wedding band. So I asked, "Why did you get married?" He said that it was because he loved his wife. I pointed out that love, in an atheistic worldview, is no different from sadness — both being chemical reactions in the brain that are essentially meaningless. Love exists in a Christian worldview where we are made in the image of a loving God.

I also pointed out that "getting married is contrary to what adherents of an evolutionary worldview teach. You have one basic goal in evolution — to pass your genes on to as many people as you can. Getting married and being faithful to one woman [which he said he was and I do want to encourage that by the way] goes against what a professed evolutionary atheist should be doing."

I continued by saying that marriage comes from the Bible, specifically in Genesis, because God created a literal man and a literal woman, hence the first marriage. After all this, the atheist just stopped to think about what we had discussed (obviously not wanting to believe it). But his hostile tone was gone, and he realized that he didn't have answers to defend his worldview. From there, we carried on a good conversation before parting ways with a handshake.

I had to neutralize his attack by pointing out contradictions in his own worldview. He assumed his view was true and was attacking the Christian view, but he was not really living out what he professed to believe. In many ways he was actually living his life as though he were a biblical Christian. I just needed to help him realize that.

Many unbelievers are used to attacking Christianity, but they are rarely required to defend their own worldview. By questioning them about it, we help them realize that their own professed worldview falls tremendously short.

Contradictions in the Unbeliever's Worldview

In our example we pointed out a few contradictions in the evolutionary atheists' worldview.

- Marriage versus no marriage
- Love being real versus love not being real
- Wearing clothes versus not wearing clothes (in public settings)

But there are a host of other problems in an atheistic worldview based on philosophical naturalism that are self-refuting. The following includes a few examples:

1. The consistent atheist says there is nothing immaterial. Those who say otherwise can't be atheists, as that would allow God, who is immaterial (John 4:24), to possibly exist. But this means that logic cannot exist either as it is immaterial (i.e., abstract). Logic has no mass and is universal (even the universe obeys the laws of logic, such as the law of non-contradiction). Being made in the image of a logical God who created and sustains the universe makes sense. Of course, many people do not perform logic correctly. That is because we have lived in a sin-cursed world ever since Genesis 3. Our fallible, imperfect minds do not always correctly "think God's thoughts after Him." But in the atheistic viewpoint, how can one maintain that there is no immaterial and yet refer to the immaterial at the same time in the same relationship?

   a. Information is immaterial, so this can't exist either.

   b. Truth is also immaterial.

   c. Love, hate, sadness, and all other emotions are immaterial.

2. The consistent atheist says the universe came from nothing, is going to nothing, and nothing matters (i.e., no purpose). So why debate the subject of God, the Bible, Christianity, and so on (why have *this* purpose)? In other words, how can one have

purpose and have no purpose at the same time in the same relationship?

3. The consistent atheist says there is no morality (since there is no God who sets an absolute standard of morality). Yet many atheists say there are some absolute moral standards, such as not to murder.[2] I recently heard an atheist say, "I don't believe in relative morality. Well I do and don't. It's great in a philosophical sense, but in practicality it doesn't always work that way. Obviously, we have universal morality such as murder is wrong." Evolutionary atheist Hitler believed murder to be acceptable,[3] as did mass murderer Jeffrey Dahmer.[4] How can one have an absolute standard and not have such a standard at the same time and in the same relationship?

4. Science comes out of a Christian worldview where God upholds the universe in a consistent fashion (e.g., Genesis 8:22; Hebrews 1:3). And God, who knows the end from the beginning (Isaiah 46:10; Revelation 22:13), has declared that this consistency will be the same in the future until the end (Genesis 8:22), so we have a basis to do science since things like the laws of nature should not change (i.e., allowing repeatable and observable science). But why would that be the case in an atheistic evolutionary worldview? How can one know things won't change tomorrow? Furthermore, how can one know that one accident could explain another accident? There is no basis for science in an atheistic worldview. How can

---

2. If an atheist really was consistent in saying there is no morality whatsoever and opted to live that way, then they are saying that it would be okay for someone to shoot them, by their own worldview because such a thing would not be wrong in that worldview. Few atheists realize the implication of their worldview. Clearly, atheism is not the correct worldview though.

3. Hitler made this clear in the first and second chapters of his second book, simply called *Hitler's Second Book*, a sequel to *Mein Kampf*.

4. "If a person doesn't think there is a God to be accountable to, then — then what's the point of trying to modify your behavior to keep it within acceptable ranges? That's how I thought anyway. I always believed the theory of evolution as truth, that we all just came from the slime. When we, when we died, you know, that was it, there is nothing." Jeffrey Dahmer, in an interview with Stone Phillips, *Dateline NBC*, Nov. 29, 1994.

one have no basis for science and yet do science? Unbelievers must borrow from the biblical worldview to make sense of the world. They must betray their professed worldview and stand on the Bible's truth to argue for atheism and oppose the Bible!

These are a few tips to utilize in a debate with people who have been duped into believing atheism and evolution. But others, such as agnostics, say that one can't know if God exists or not. But how can they know that? How can these people who claim that "one really cannot know anything for certain" be certain about not being able to know about God? Empiricists say that all truth claims must come from our senses, but when has *that truth claim* ever been confirmed by our senses?

This method works with all religious perspectives, even those that incorporate Christianity in their beliefs while mixing it with other beliefs (like those who mix evolution and millions of years, which are subsets of the religion of humanism, with the Bible). For more good questions to ask, please consult *The New Answers Book 3*, chapter 30 by Dr. Jason Lisle and Mike Riddle.[5]

Conclusion

Pointing out supposed contradictions in the Bible is really nothing more than a smoke screen to keep people distracted from the real issue — the numerous contradictions in the humanistic worldview. The sad thing is that skeptics don't realize it is just a smoke screen. Not only are they blinded from the truth of God's Word, but they also have a tendency to be blinded to the contradictions and inconsistencies of their own worldview. Scripture refers to such people as those "whose minds the god of this age has blinded, who do not believe" (2 Corinthians 4:4).

As we have said in our many articles, our books, and our website (www.answersingenesis.org), the Bible cannot and does not contain any legitimate contradictions or inconsistencies. It is infallible in its original autographs. When we place our faith on Christ and trust His

---

5. Ken Ham, general editor, *The New Answers Book 3* (Green Forest, AR: Master Books, 2010).

Word, we build for ourselves a firm foundation (Matthew 7:24–27) rooted in truth. This truth is absolute, and it allows us to make sense of logic, morals, ethics, the human condition (sin), death, suffering, science, and everything else in the world around us. If the Bible is not true, then logic and morals would have no basis.[6]

One of the main things we must remember when reading Scripture is that, whether saved or not, we still live in sinful human bodies. We still read God's Word with fallible limited minds, skewed perceptions, and broken emotions. Our first reaction to something we don't understand might be to say, "Is this a contradiction?" or maybe, "This can't be right." But we need to keep in mind that we are reading words that are God-breathed and infallible. Even though we may not immediately see the solution, we must have faith that it does exist.

At the same time, we must carefully examine each instance, rather than jumping to accept potentially dubious solutions. Even with good intentions, some explanations just make it worse. For example, it does not help the case of inerrancy to say that the details are wrong, but only the big picture matters.

So what are we to do? First, we need to remember God's Word is perfect and relevant in all areas of life (2 Timothy 3:15–17; 2 Peter 1:3). We are sinful, imperfect human beings (Romans 3:23). The correct approach would be to state, "How am I misunderstanding these two passages?" With further study of the Scriptures, guidance from Holy Spirit, and a desire to uncover the truth, you will likely find the answer.

But for humanists, no matter what sort of mental gymnastics they try to perform they will never be able to reconcile, explain, or make sense of the contradictions within their own worldview. So as you read this book and as you live every day, keep in mind the words of Psalm 118:8, which states, "It is better to trust in the LORD than to put confidence in man."

---

6. For more on how these things only make sense in the Christian worldview, please read Dr. Jason Lisle's book, *The Ultimate Proof of Creation*.

Genesis

Planting Confusion

← Tim Chaffey →

Were plants created on day 3 or day 6?

The "Problem"

Critics have charged that the first two chapters of the Bible contain a contradiction regarding the creation of the vegetation. Some old-earth creationists have pointed to the same passages to bolster their claim that the early chapters of Genesis need not be interpreted as historical narrative. The passages are found in Genesis 1 and 2:

Then God said, "Let the earth bring forth grass, the herb that yields seed, and the fruit tree that yields fruit according to its kind, whose seed is in itself, on the earth"; and it was so. And the earth brought forth grass, the herb that yields seed according to its kind, and the tree that yields fruit, whose seed is in itself according to its kind. And God saw that it was good. So the evening and the morning were the third day (Genesis 1:11–13).

This is the history of the heavens and the earth when they were created, in the day that the LORD God made the earth and the heavens, before any plant of the field was in the earth and before any herb of the field had grown. For the LORD God had not caused it to rain on the earth, and there was no man to till the ground; but a mist went up from the earth and watered the whole face of the ground.

And the LORD God formed man of the dust of the ground, and breathed into his nostrils the breath of life; and man became a living being. The LORD God planted a garden eastward in Eden, and there He put the man whom He had formed. And out of the ground the LORD God made every tree grow that is pleasant to the sight and good for food. The tree of life was also in the midst of the garden, and the tree of the knowledge of good and evil (Genesis 2:4–9).

The Solution

There is a rather simple solution to this alleged contradiction. On the third day of the creation week, God made certain types of plants: "grass, the herb that yields seed, and the fruit tree" (Genesis 1:11). Each of these terms translates specific Hebrew terms for grass (*deshe'*), the seed-yielding herbs (*'eseb mazria zera*), and the fruit trees (*ets pariy*).

Beginning with the fourth verse of Genesis 2, the writer zooms in on the events of the sixth day. God made Adam (v. 7), the Garden of Eden along with the plants therein (specifically mentioned are the fruit trees, v. 8–9), and Eve (v. 22).

What about the plants described in verse 5? Why weren't those created on day 3 when God made the other plants? The context provides the answer. Verses 5 and 6 provide a description of what the world was like prior to the creation of man. Two specific types of plants are translated from specific Hebrew terms: "plant of the field" (*siah hassadeh*) and "herb of the field" (*eseb hassadeh*). Hebrew scholar Mark Futato defines these terms as "wild shrubs of the steppe" and "cultivated grain," respectively.[1]

This verse is preparing the reader for what is going to happen next in the narrative. The cultivated *herbs of the field* were not around because Adam had not been created yet, so there was no one to till or cultivate the ground. The "wild shrubs of the steppe" are plants that often have thorns, and those with thorns would not have been present until after the Curse.[2]

---

1. Mark Futato, "Because It Had Rained: A Study of Genesis 2:5–7 with Implications for Genesis 2:4–25 and Genesis 1:1–2:3." *Westminster Theological Journal*, 60:1–21 (Spring 1998): 4. It may not be the best practice to identify something as "wild" prior to the Fall, but the definition given here is based on how the term is commonly understood — not just before sin.

2. Kenneth L. Gentry and Michael R. Butler, *Yea, Hath God Said?* (Eugene, OR: Wipf and Stock Publishers, 2002), p. 91.

While announcing the Curse, God said to Adam, "Cursed is the ground for your sake; in toil you shall eat of it all the days of your life. Both *thorns* and *thistles* it shall bring forth for you, and you shall eat the *herb of the field*. In the sweat of your face you shall eat bread till you return to the ground, for out of it you were taken; for dust you are, and to dust you shall return" (Genesis 3:17–19, emphasis added).

As a result of the Curse, Adam would no longer have it easy. Instead of eating the abundance of fruit from the trees in the garden, he would need to till the ground and grow crops for food.[3] This would be hard work, because the ground was now going to produce thorns and thistles.

Conclusion

A closer look at the text reveals there is no contradiction. In Genesis 2:5–6 the writer set up the narrative and informed the reader of what was to come. These verses provide a description of the world on day 6 before God created Adam. The grasses, fruit trees, and seed-yielding herbs were created on day 3 (with the exception of those within the garden), but the thorny plants and cultivated grains came about after Adam was created.

---

3. Genesis 2:15 does state that Adam was put in the garden to "tend and keep it." The word *tend* likely refers to cultivation, but this still fits within the proposed solution since Genesis 2:5 states that the "herb of the field" had not grown yet since it had not rained and "there was no man to till the ground."

Eve's Birth Certificate

❧ Mariah Smith ☙

Was Eve created on day 6 or not?

The "Problem"

Genesis 1 and 2 seem to indicate different times for the creation of Eve. Here are the relevant passages:

> So God created man in His own image; in the image of God He created him; male and female He created them. Then God blessed them, and God said to them, "Be fruitful and multiply; fill the earth and subdue it; have dominion over the fish of the sea, over the birds of the air, and over every living thing that moves on the earth." And God said, "See, I have given you every herb that yields seed which is on the face of all the earth, and every tree whose fruit yields seed; to you it shall be for food. Also, to every beast of the earth, to every bird of the air, and to everything that creeps on the earth, in which there is life, I have given every green herb for food"; and it was so. Then God saw everything that He had made, and indeed it was very good. So the evening and the morning were the sixth day (Genesis 1:27–31).

> So Adam gave names to all cattle, to the birds of the air, and to every beast of the field. But for Adam there was not found a helper comparable to him. And the LORD God caused a deep sleep to fall on Adam, and he slept; and He took one of his ribs, and closed up the flesh in its place. Then the rib which the LORD God had taken from man He made into a woman, and He brought her to the man (Genesis 2:20–22).

According to Genesis 1:27, God created the first male and female on day 6. Eve was even called the mother of all the living

(Genesis 3:20). How could this be true if she was not created until the events of Genesis 2:20–22? Isn't this a clear contradiction?

The Solution

People may think the creation of Eve happened later, because the Bible doesn't go into full detail about Eve's creation until Genesis 2. However, if you look at Genesis 1:27–31, you find that God created both Adam and Eve on day 6 (male *and female*). Genesis 2:7–25 provides more detail about the sixth day of creation than Genesis 1:24–31 does. The fact that they're both actually describing the same events easily explains any alleged contradiction.

We need to read carefully and not add our own ideas into the Bible. For example, some people claim that Adam couldn't have possibly named all the living creatures in one day, so they think the creation of Eve, which occurred after this event, had to take place later. However, Genesis 2:20 says, "Adam gave names to all cattle, to the birds of the air, and to every beast of the field." It doesn't say anything about his naming sea creatures or creeping things.

Also, "all cattle," and "every beast of the field" (Genesis 2:20) may not mean the same thing as every "beast of the earth" (Genesis 1:24); it was probably a smaller set that represented all types of beasts of the earth. Adam only named the animals God brought to him, and besides, he had most of the day to do it. Before the Fall, Adam's brain was perfect, so he shouldn't have had problems coming up with names. It has been estimated that only a few hours would be needed to name the animals.[1]

Conclusion

So Adam had plenty of time to name all the animals God brought to him — leaving plenty of time for Eve's creation on the same day. Eve was created on day 6, just like the first two chapters of the Bible say.

---

1. See next section, "Not Enough Hours in the Day," for more details on how all of the events on day 6 could have taken place within the allotted time.

Not Enough Hours in the Day

← Tim Chaffey →

Could the events of day 6 have fit within 24 hours?

The "Problem"

In an effort to show the days of the creation week should not be interpreted as 24-hour days, several old-earth creationists have argued that the events of day 6 could not have fit within a single day. Skeptics and critics have used the same argument in their attempts to find contradictions in Scripture. The late old-earth creationist Dr. Gleason Archer summarized the problem this way:

> We are told that God created Adam first, gave him the responsibility of tending the Garden of Eden *for some time* until He observed him to be lonely. He then granted him the fellowship of *all the beasts and animals of earth*, with opportunity to bestow names upon them *all*. Some *undetermined period after* that, God observed that Adam *was still lonely* and *finally* fashioned a human wife for him by means of a rib removed from him during a "deep sleep." Then at last he brought Eve before Adam and presented her to him as his new life partner. Who can imagine that all of these transactions could possibly have taken place *in 120 minutes* of the sixth day (or even within twenty-four hours, for that matter)? And yet *Gen. 1:27 states that both Adam and Eve were created at the very end of the final day of creation.* Obviously the "days" of chapter 1 are intended to represent stages of unspecified length, not literal twenty-four-hour days.[1] (emphasis added)

---

1. Gleason Archer, *A Survey of Old Testament Introduction* (Chicago, IL: Moody Press, 1994, 3rd ed.), p. 201.

The well-respected Christian apologist Dr. Norman Geisler, built upon this argument by stating that God's statement, "I will make a helper suitable for him" (Genesis 2:18 NIV), implies a period of time between the proclamation and the actual performance. He also wrote that "Adam indicated he had anticipated Eve for some time" before she was created.[2]

The Solution

This alleged contradiction gives us a perfect opportunity to look closely at the text instead of relying on someone's retelling of the passage. With all due respect to Dr. Archer and Dr. Geisler, their claims do not line up with Scripture. When we read Genesis 1–2 and compare it to the quote from Dr. Archer, we notice something very interesting. I have highlighted various sections of the quote above, because the italics represent ideas not found in the text. Instead, they were inserted into the text by Dr. Archer. Notice that each of these additions inserts timing elements into the passage. He used terms such as "for some time," "all the beasts and animals of earth," "still lonely," "finally," "120 minutes," and "at the very end of the final day of creation."

Let's look at what the Bible actually teaches on each of these subjects.

> Then the LORD God took the man and put him in the garden of Eden to tend and keep it. And the LORD God commanded the man, saying, "Of every tree of the garden you may freely eat; but of the tree of the knowledge of good and evil you shall not eat, for in the day that you eat of it you shall surely die."
>
> And the LORD God said, "It is not good that man should be alone; I will make him a helper comparable to him." Out of the ground the LORD God formed every beast of the field and every bird of the air, and brought them to Adam to see what he would call them. And whatever Adam called each living creature, that was its name. So Adam gave names to all cattle, to the birds of

---

2. Norman L. Geisler, *Systematic Theology*, Vol. 2 (Minneapolis, MN: Bethany House, 2003), p. 643.

the air, and to every beast of the field. But for Adam there was not found a helper comparable to him.

And the LORD God caused a deep sleep to fall on Adam, and he slept; and He took one of his ribs, and closed up the flesh in its place. Then the rib which the LORD God had taken from man He made into a woman, and He brought her to the man.

And Adam said:
"This is now bone of my bones
And flesh of my flesh;
She shall be called Woman,
Because she was taken out of Man" (Genesis 2:15–23).

The Bible does not tell us that Adam tended the garden "for some time," nor does it imply that he tended the garden at all prior to naming the animals. The Bible simply tells us that tending the garden was a reason God put Adam in the garden. It does not give us any indication whether or not he had already started working. Scripture never states that all of these events happened within "120 minutes," and Genesis 1:27 does not tell us that "Adam and Eve were created at the very end of the final day of creation." Rather, it states, "So God created man in His own image; in the image of God He created him; male and female He created them."

Perhaps the most difficult aspect of this objection is related to the naming of the animals. How could Adam possibly have named all of the animals in one day? I previously dealt with this issue in another work. Concerning the naming of animals, I wrote:

First, the text does not state that Adam had "fellowship" with and named "all the beasts and animals of the earth." This is a common misunderstanding on the part of the old-earthers, due to a failure to observe the text carefully. According to verse 20, Adam only named the cattle, beasts of the field, and birds of the air. He was not responsible for naming the sea creatures, the beasts of the earth or creeping things (insects, etc.). This would considerably reduce the amount of animals that he had to name. It has been demonstrated that Adam could have easily named each of these creatures in less than four hours, while taking a five-minute break every hour![3]

Dr. Geisler's comments are not demanded by Scripture either. The fact that God said He would make a helper for Adam does not imply that much time passed from the proclamation of the words to the actual creation of Eve. God could have put Adam into a deep sleep immediately after Adam named the animals. Also, Adam's response to the creation of Eve does not imply that he had waited for her for a considerable amount of time. This claim is based on Genesis 2:23, which in some translations have Adam proclaim, "This at last is bone of my bones and flesh of my flesh" (ESV). The Hebrew word, rendered as "at last" in the ESV and "now" in most translations, is פַּעַם (pa'am), and it refers to "an event which happens in a time sequence, with reference to other points in time."[4] So either translation is fine, but neither one proves Geisler's point. Adam had already named the animals and fallen into a deep sleep, so there is no reason to believe that his use of the word "pa'am" would imply a long period of time. Imagine working an eight-hour shift, and when five o'clock comes around, you proclaim, "At last, I can go home." No one would think that you've been at work for more than a day.

So let's look at a plausible time-line of events for the sixth day using the information from Genesis 1–2. Remember, Genesis 2 focuses on events of day 6, while Genesis 1 gives us a brief overview of that day. For the sake of argument, let's assume that Adam actually did tend the garden for some time and that God only worked during the 12-hour daylight portion of the day.

---

3. Tim Chaffey and Jason Lisle, *Old-Earth Creationism on Trial: The Verdict Is In* (Green Forest, AR: Master Books, 2008), p. 69. The information referenced in this quote concerning the naming of the animals is Andrew Kulikovsky, "How Could Adam Have Named All the Animals in a Single Day?" *Creation* 27:3 (June 2005), p. 27–28.

4. James Swanson, *Dictionary of Biblical Languages with Semantic Domains: Hebrew (Old Testament),* electronic ed. (Bellingham, WA: Logos Research Systems, Inc., 1997).

6:00–7:00	God creates land animals
7:00–8:00	God creates Adam from dust
8:00–9:00	God creates the garden and puts Adam in it
9:00–11:00	Adam tends the garden
11:00–3:00	Adam names the animals
3:00–5:00	Adam sleeps, and God creates Eve from Adam's rib
5:00–6:00	Adam and Eve meet, and God tells them what they should and shouldn't eat

Of course, there is no reason why it would take God an hour to create the land animals and another hour for the creation of Adam. The omnipotent God could have performed each of these actions instantaneously.

Conclusion

The Bible does not give too many details to fit into 24 hours on the sixth day. In fact, all of the activities described for each of the days of the creation week could easily have been accomplished within 12 hours of the respective days. It is only when one adds timing elements to the text that the sixth day seems to describe too many events.

There is no contradiction on this issue, but it does highlight the problem of trying to add fallible man's opinions to the text. Some seemingly well-intentioned Christians have attempted to harmonize God's Word with the ever-changing opinions of man, yet this practice ends up adding more problems than it allegedly solves. God has given us His inspired and inerrant Word, and we can be confident that it does not contradict itself.

Could Adam Eat from Any Tree?

⟵ Bodie Hodge ⟶

Did God contradict Himself concerning what He said Adam could eat?

The "Problem"

God said that Adam and Eve may eat from *any* tree in Genesis 1, but in Genesis 2 He said that they may not eat from one tree.

> And God said, "See, I have given you every herb that yields seed which is on the face of all the earth, and every tree whose fruit yields seed; to you it shall be for food" (Genesis 1:29).

> And the LORD God commanded the man, saying, "Of every tree of the garden you may freely eat; but of the tree of the knowledge of good and evil you shall not eat, for in the day that you eat of it you shall surely die" (Genesis 2:16–17).

This seems to be a rather straightforward contradiction. God said to eat and not to eat; however, there are several possible solutions that easily reveal this is not a contradiction.

The Solution

One possibility is revealed by reading these two verses more carefully. There are qualifying terms in Genesis 1:29 that show the herbs and fruit must produce seeds. So, potentially, there were trees and herbs that did not produce seed and were off-limits.

Consider for a moment that some plants reproduce by other means — shoots, sprouts, and so on. Even some "fruited" vegetation use these other means of spreading in addition to seeds. Raspberries, for example, lean over and strike the ground, and roots develop for the next year's plants. Strawberries send out shoots that also take root. But they still reproduce via fruit and seed, so they would have been allowed.

The fruit of figs have seeds, so they too would be included as edible food per Genesis 1:29, and indeed, figs were found in the Garden of Eden (Genesis 3:7). So consider for a moment how this alleged contradiction "bears no fruit" if the fruit of the tree of the knowledge of good and evil had no seed in it. This would resolve the proposed contradiction.

But there are other potential solutions that could eliminate this alleged contradiction. The Lord could have been speaking of the fruit on the face of the whole earth beyond the special and unique Garden of Eden. This would make sense considering there were special instructions given to Adam regarding what was edible in the Garden and what was not. In other words, they may have been complementary commands given for two different places.

This information would prove rather useful had they traveled beyond the borders of the Garden for expedition of potential living space for their descendants. Remember, they were commanded to be fruitful and fill the earth in Genesis 1:28. So knowing that edible food was ready for them beyond the Garden would only make filling the earth that much easier.

Probably the simplest explanation is that the command about not eating from the tree of knowledge of good and evil was given first and served as an exception clause. Although it appears in the Bible in Genesis 2:17, this instruction was delivered prior to the creation of Eve. In Genesis 1, God's instruction about food occurred after the creation of Eve, so Adam was already fully aware of the exception.

These types of exceptions appear elsewhere in Scripture. For example, Jesus gave an exception in Matthew 5:32 and Matthew 19:9 regarding divorce. So assuming that giving an exception clause is without warrant would be inaccurate. It simply shows that God revealed more information about a particular subject at the necessary time.

Conclusion

Any of these possibilities indicate that this alleged contradiction can be "pruned from the tree." Once again, the Bible easily withstands the attack of the skeptic.

Times of Recession

❖ Michael Belknap ❖

When was the earth dry after the Flood of Noah's day?

The "Problem"

It is alleged that verses 13 and 14 in the eighth chapter of Genesis are contradictory. Critics assert that two different dates are given for when the earth was dry after the global Flood. Consider the following:

> And it came to pass in the six hundred and first year, in *the first month, the first day of the month*, that the waters were dried up from the earth; and Noah removed the covering of the ark and looked, and indeed the surface of the ground was dry. And in *the second month, on the twenty-seventh day of the month*, the earth was dried (Genesis 8:13–14, emphasis added).

So how could the earth dry up on both of these dates?

The Solution

All forms of human communication contain inherent limitations (Genesis 11:1–9). Because of these limitations, properly translating words and concepts from one language into another language can be a difficult task. In light of this, it is advisable to examine Scriptures in their original languages — especially when allegations of corruption or contradiction arise.

Consider, for instance, that the word translated as "dried" and "dry" in verse 13 is a different Hebrew word than what is rendered "dried" in verse 14. Don't let me scare you too much with Hebrew words, but the phrase "were dried up from off the earth" uses the word *charab* (translated as "dried"). The phrase "and, behold, the face of the ground was dry" once again uses the Hebrew word *charab*. Compare this to verse 14 where the word for "dried" is *yabesh*.

Charab in this form means "to be waste" and "be desolate," while *yabesh* in this form means "to be dry" and "be without moisture."

This language indicates that a gradient of drying has occurred, and it is clearly not a restatement of the same degree or concept of dryness. Therefore, the use of *charab* in this context indicates that the Flood waters had largely drained from the continents, though the ground would have still been saturated. *Yabesh*, on the other hand, indicates that continents were truly dry near the end of the following month.

Another consideration is the probable change in location of the observer. There seems to be a shift in perspective moving from verse 13 to 14. Verse 13 states that from Noah's point of reference atop the ark, the surface of the ground appeared dry on the first day of the first month. Verse 14 seems to indicate that the declaration of the earth being sufficiently dry 56 days later came from God's perspective, since only He would have known this information.[1] Since the ark came to rest amongst the "mountains of Ararat" (Genesis 8:4), it is expected that the elevated region within eyesight of Noah dried sooner than other lower areas.

Finally, and perhaps most obviously, it is rather arrogant of the critic to think the writer of Genesis was so ignorant that he couldn't keep from contradicting himself in two successive verses. Rather than immediately charging the writer with a contradiction, these individuals should dig a little deeper. Instead, in their haste to find problems in Scripture, those who claim these verses to be contradictory end up looking foolish for failing to understand the basic uses of language.

Conclusion

With all of this in mind, we can confidently conclude that these back-to-back verses contain no legitimate contradiction. This example is a reminder that it is crucial to understand both context and language when discerning an author's intent of communication.

---

1. Bodie Hodge explained in his *Biblical Overview of the Flood Timeline*. "From the first day of the year during the daylight portion there were 29.5 more days left in the month plus 26.5 more days left in the second month until the exit." Adding 29.5 days to 26.5 days equals 56 days. Before the Flood and sometime after, it seems that a 360-day year was observed; thus, a 30-day month is applied in this calculation.

Who Destroyed Sodom?

← Tommy Mitchell →

In Genesis 19:13, two angels claim they would destroy Sodom, but verse 24 records that the Lord destroyed it.

The "Problem"

After the Lord Himself and two angels appear to Abraham in Genesis 18, the two angels traveled to Sodom to warn Lot and his family. They told Lot, "For we will destroy this place . . . the LORD has sent us to destroy it" (Genesis 19:13). Later, verse 24 states, "Then the LORD rained brimstone and fire on Sodom and Gomorrah, from the LORD out of the heavens."

The Solution

Notice that after hearing the warning from the angels that they would destroy the city, Lot told his family members, "The LORD will destroy this city." Clearly, Lot understood the angels to be acting as agents of God under His authority. Thus, whatever role the angels would have in the coming destruction, the Lord's judgment and power were ultimately responsible.

The principle of delegation means that when one in authority commands an action, he can rightly be given credit for it, even if he has an agent perform the action. In this case, God delegated the announcement of destruction to the angels. The principle holds true because God is the one with the power to enable the action and authority to order it.

Scripture contains other examples like this. For instance, Matthew 19:8 records Jesus attributing the rules about divorce to Moses, and in John 7:19 Jesus says, "Did not Moses give you the law?" However, Scripture is clear that God gave Moses the law, both the commandments written on tablets of stone (moral) and the additional laws, which elaborated on the law and regulated society (civil) and ceremony.

In our modern language, we speak the same way. When a platoon of soldiers destroys an enemy facility, we can rightly say the platoon did it, or the general giving the command did it, or the president did it, or the United States did it.

Similarly, the Bible contains instances where a leader other than God is credited with work that was actually performed by someone in His command. For example, Moses stated, "So I made an ark of acacia wood" (Deuteronomy 10:3), but Exodus 37:1 states, "Then Bezalel made the ark of acacia wood." Bezalel was the actual craftsman who built the ark of the covenant, but it was under the command of Moses, so it is perfectly legitimate for either man to be given credit.

In the case of Sodom and Gomorrah, God sent the angels as His emissaries to Lot. They acted on His behalf. In fact, God even said to Abraham, "Because the outcry against Sodom and Gomorrah is great, and because their sin is very grave, I will go down now and see" (Genesis 18:20–21). At that point, the angels went to Sodom, but the Lord stayed behind and talked with Abraham. So sending the angels to act on His behalf was viewed by God as being the same as going there Himself. This is yet another example of the aforementioned principle in action. Since the angels acted on God's behalf, we can safely say they had some part in carrying out the judgment.

We know that God doesn't need help to do anything. After all, He spoke the entire universe into existence in all its details. In creation, we know that all persons of the Trinity were involved. But there are also many places where God chooses to use angels, men, or even animals to accomplish His purpose. Throughout Scripture, angels delivered messages, carried out judgments, and ministered to the heirs of salvation. Thus, it should be no surprise to learn that angels were instrumental in carrying out this destruction.

Conclusion

The angels did it — or at least some of it. And the Lord did it. Both are true, so there is no contradiction.

A "Sonny" Day

← Bodie Hodge →

Did Abraham have one son or more than one?

The "Problem"

I once had a hostile person call me and attack the Bible by saying it was full of contradictions. So I kindly asked him to name one. At that point, he fumbled for an answer for a while (I think he had to find something to reference). Eventually, he said the Bible was in error when Abraham was told to sacrifice his son, because the Bible says it was his *only* son, Isaac, but that could not be true because of Isaac's older brother, Ishmael.

I responded, "Let's look it up, because the way you stated it sounds like a contradiction. It is true that Ishmael was Isaac's older brother [Genesis 16:11], but I would rather see what the Bible actually says."

At first, he was offended that I didn't take his word for it. And this a good lesson in itself. Why trust what someone says God says, when we can easily read God's Word for ourselves?

So I turned to Genesis 22 and read the following words:

> Then He said, "Take now your son, your only son Isaac, whom you love, and go to the land of Moriah, and offer him there as a burnt offering on one of the mountains of which I shall tell you" (Genesis 22:2).

The passage didn't say exactly what the caller had claimed. There are a number of answers to this alleged contradiction. My initial response was to point out the phrase "whom you love" as a qualifier for "your only son." In other words, Isaac was the only son Abraham truly loved, being the son of the wife he loved and being the child of promise.

So I told the caller that there was no contradiction here, since the Bible says Abraham had only one son *that he loved*. The caller replied, "You Christians are clever!"

Did Abraham not love Ishmael? Well the Bible simply doesn't say. It's true that he listened to Sarah and sent Ishmael and his mother, Hagar, away. But Abraham was originally distressed by this plan. God told him, "Do not let it be displeasing in your sight because of the lad or because of your bondwoman. Whatever Sarah has said to you, listen to her voice; for in Isaac your seed shall be called. Yet I will also make a nation of the bondwoman, because he is your seed" (Genesis 21:12–13). This was the second time God had promised Abraham that Ishmael would be blessed. In the first instance, Abraham asked God to make Ishmael the son of promise (Genesis 17:18–20). So Abraham obviously cared for Ishmael, but his affection for Ishmael paled in comparison to his immense love for Isaac.

The Solution

When I look back on this conversation, I realize that I could have given him a few different responses, and that is especially so now that I have studied the subject in more detail. Since then, I have considered other relevant passages such as the following:

> By faith Abraham, when he was tested, offered up Isaac, and he who had received the promises offered up his only begotten son, of whom it was said, "In Isaac your seed shall be called," concluding that God was able to raise him up, even from the dead, from which he also received him in a figurative sense (Hebrews 11:17–19).

The passage in Hebrews qualifies the "only son" concept as well. Isaac was the *only begotten* (i.e., unique, special) son of Abraham. Isaac was indeed unique and special in that he was the promised son through whom Jesus Christ, the Messiah, would come (Genesis 17:19–21).

Similarly, Jesus Christ is the *only begotten* Son of God (John 3:16), even though others are called the sons of God (e.g., Adam in Luke 3:38 and Christians in Galatians 3:26). Jesus is the only *unique and special* Son of God — God who became a man.

This brings up another answer to the alleged contradiction. The Hebrew word used for "only" is *yachiyd*, which means "unique" or "only begotten" (special). So the Hebrew clarifies that Isaac is indeed the special, unique, only begotten son of Abraham. Isaac was the son of promise. So this answers the alleged contradiction.

Sometimes we miss the obvious answer as well. In the previous chapter (Genesis 21), Ishmael was sent away. So in chapter 22, Isaac was Abraham's only son, for his other had gone away, presumably never to return under Abraham's household. So this is another plausible solution to the alleged contradiction. Also, once Isaac had grown and Sarah had died, Abraham married Keturah, and they had six sons together (Genesis 25:1–2).

Conclusion

This answer highlights two important practices in dealing with the alleged contradictions in Scripture. First, make sure you take the time to read the relevant passages to make sure the one making the charge is accurately quoting the Bible. Second, remember that you don't have to answer right away, especially if you haven't studied the subject before. This is a little more difficult during a phone conversation, but it is crucial to take the time to explore the Scriptures so you can give an accurate response. Nevertheless, there is no contradiction about the number of Abraham's sons.

An Important Side Note

Some see this passage and think God is rather inhumane because He asked Abraham to sacrifice his son. For those unfamiliar with the passage, Abraham was about to kill Isaac when the Lord stopped him. The Lord tested him, and Abraham demonstrated his tremendous faithfulness in that he would not withhold from God his only begotten son, whom he loved.

Abraham's faith in the Lord was extraordinary (Hebrews 11:17) because he knew that the Lord would fulfill His promises about Isaac and his descendants (Genesis 17:19). He knew the Lord had power over life and death. For example, he rhetorically asked in Genesis 18:14, "Is anything too hard for the LORD?" Referring to himself and Isaac, Abraham told his servants that "we will come back" from the sacrifice (Genesis 22:5). He also told Isaac, "God will provide for Himself the lamb for a burnt offering" (Genesis 22:8). So Abraham trusted that the Lord could bring Isaac back to life, if necessary.

This event served as an incredible foreshadowing of Christ's sacrifice on the Cross. The Lord God sent His only begotten Son, Jesus Christ, whom He loved (Luke 3:22) to die for us sinners (Romans 5:8). God raised Him from the dead on the third day (Acts 10:39–40). Jesus does indeed possess the keys to death (Revelation 1:18).

Interestingly, the Lord sent Abraham to a mountain in the land of Moriah to sacrifice his only begotten son, Isaac (Genesis 22:2). Approximately 1,000 years later, Solomon built the temple on Mt. Moriah in Jerusalem (2 Chronicles 3:1), which is the very city where Jesus Christ was sacrificed on the Cross.

Exodus~
Deuteronomy

What Is God's Name in the Old Testament?

← Bodie Hodge →

God was known by several names in the Old Testament (Elohim, Jehovah, and El Shaddai in Exodus 6:2–3; Jealous in Exodus 34:14; and I AM WHO I AM in Exodus 3:14). Which one is accurate?

I am sometimes surprised at how easy it is to answer some alleged Bible contradictions. And this one is rather easy. Imagine if someone came up to me and said, "What is your name? Is it Bodie or Mr. Hodge?" Well, the answer is simple: it is both.

Should we assume that God has only one name and all others are contradictions in Scripture? That would be absurd. God often gave new names to people, such as Jacob becoming Israel or Abram becoming Abraham and so on. The names have meaning, too. For example, Abram means "exalted father" and Abraham means "the father of a multitude." The latter name obviously reflected the promise God made to Abraham about having countless offspring (e.g., Genesis 17:5–6). So having more than one name is no contradiction at all.

God often revealed things by the name He gave for Himself. For example, Jehovah-Jireh means "the LORD provides." In fact, the name Jehovah is derived from YHWH, the name God revealed to Moses. It is from a root word translated as "I AM" in the title "I AM WHO I AM" (Exodus 3:14). This helps us understand that God is the ultimate authority in all matters at all times and existence is predicated upon Him. In fact, there are a number of names that God reveals to us in Scripture. Here are some from the Old Testament:

Some Old Testament Names of God (not exhaustive)[1]

	Name	Brief meaning	Reference
1	Elohim	God (Majestic plural yet used with singular verbs for God)	Genesis 1:1
2	El	God (singular)	Genesis 7:1
3	El Shaddai	God is sufficient/almighty	Genesis 17:1
4	El Elyon	God Most High	Deuteronomy 26:19
5	El Roi	God sees	Genesis 16:13
6	El Olam	God everlasting	Genesis 21:33
7	El Gibbor	Mighty God	Isaiah 9:6
8	Jehovah	"I AM WHO I AM" or Yahweh or "to be"; In English Bibles translated as "LORD"	Genesis 2:4 (Jehovah Elohim specifically here)
9	Jehovah-Magen	The LORD my shield	Psalm 3:3
10	Jehovah-Tsaddiq	The LORD is righteous	2 Chronicles 12:6
11	Jehovah-Jireh	The LORD provides or the Lord sees	Genesis 22:14
12	Jehovah-Rapha	The LORD heals	Exodus 15:26
13	Jehovah-Nissi	The LORD is our banner	Exodus 17:15
14	Jehovah-M'Kaddesh	The LORD sanctifies	Leviticus 20:7
15	Jehovah-Shalom	The LORD is our peace	Judges 6:24
16	Jehovah-Rohi	The LORD is our shepherd	Psalm 23:1
17	Jehovah-Shammah	The LORD is there	Ezekiel 48:35
18	Jehovah-Sabaoth	LORD of hosts	Isaiah 1:24
19	Jehovah-Tsidkenu	The LORD is our righteousness	Jeremiah 23:5
20	Jehovah-Hoseenu (Asah)	The LORD our Maker	Psalm 95:6
21	Judge (Shaphat)	The Judge	Genesis 18:25
22	Mighty One (Abir)	Mighty One	Genesis 49:24
23	Branch (Tsemach)	The Branch	Jeremiah 23:5
24	Holy One (Kadosh)	Holy One	2 Kings 19:22
25	Jealous (Kanna)	Jealous	Exodus 34:14

1. Note that in some cases there are variant spellings because they have been transliterated from Hebrew into English.

26	Deliverer (Palet) or (Rhuomai Greek)	Deliverer	2 Samuel 22:2 and Romans 11:26
27	Savior (Yeshua)	Savior	Isaiah 43:3
28	Redeemer (Ga'al)	Redeemer	Job 19:25
29	Shepherd (Ra'ah)	The Shepherd, overseer	Genesis 49:24
30	Stone (Eben) of Israel	Stone	Genesis 49:24
31	Strength (Eyaluwth)	Strength	Psalm 22:19
32	Adonai	Master or Lord (as plural); in English Bibles translated as "Lord"	Genesis 15:2
33	Rock (Tsur) of Israel	Rock	Isaiah 30:29
34	King (Melekh)	King	Isaiah 41:21 [of Israel]; Psalm 74:12
35	Father (Ab) or (Abba Greek)	Father	Malachi 1:6 and Galatians 4:6
36	First (Ri'shon) and Last (Acharon) or (Protos and Eschatos in Greek)	First and Last	Isaiah 48:12 and Revelation 1:11
37	Immanuel	God with us	Isaiah 7:14

Livestock or "Deadstock"?

✦ Troy Lacey ✦

Did the fifth plague kill all of the Egyptian livestock or not?

The "Problem"

Exodus 9:6 states, "So the LORD did this thing on the next day, and all the livestock of Egypt died; but of the livestock of the children of Israel, not one died."

This verse indicates that the fifth plague on Egypt destroyed all of the livestock in that country. Yet Exodus 9:20–25 has livestock in Egypt being protected in houses from the seventh plague. How could Egyptian livestock be protected if it had all been killed earlier in the chapter?

The Solution

There are at least six reasonable explanations for this apparent contradiction, and it is quite possible that more than one of these is correct to a lesser or greater extent. If one or more of these solutions is correct then the alleged contradiction is eliminated.

First, Exodus 9:3 states, "Behold, the hand of the LORD will be on your cattle in the field, on the horses, on the donkeys, on the camels, on the oxen, and on the sheep — a very severe pestilence." Surprisingly, this verse does not mention one of the most important domestic animals at that time — the goat.[1] Therefore, it is possible that all of the livestock except goats were killed in the first plague on the livestock (fifth plague overall), and in the second instance it was goats that were affected by the plague of hail.

---

1. The NIV is the only version that translates the Hebrew *tso'n* as "goat" while every other major version translates it as "sheep" or "flocks" which matches the way it is translated in the majority of occurrences throughout Scripture. The typical words used for goats are *gedi*, *'ez*, or *sa'iyr*, none of which appear in Exodus 9:3.

Second, Exodus 9:19–20 mentions that those who "feared the word of the LORD among the servants of Pharaoh" were told to get their livestock out of the fields. Some scholars mention that these Egyptians may have been warned about the previous plague of pestilence (although it was not recorded), so *they* still had all of their livestock left. In this scenario, God warned them to put all of their livestock in barns so they wouldn't be killed by hail.

The third possibility is similar to the previous explanation except that the survival of their livestock hinges on the phrase "servants of Pharaoh." Perhaps this means they were not actually Egyptians, but other vassal subjects who were warned of the plagues so that their animals could be spared. So in Exodus 9:6, where it says that all the livestock of Egypt died, this view suggests that the animals belonging to these foreign vassals were spared if they obeyed God and not Pharaoh.

Fourth, the Bible does not reveal how much time passed between the fifth plague and the seventh plague. Following the fifth plague, which wiped out the livestock of Egypt, the Egyptians may have taken some of the livestock belonging to Israel. Another possibility is that they bought (or took) livestock from surrounding areas (Libya, Ethiopia, Canaan, etc.). The first option would require very little time to complete while the second would probably require at least a few weeks. But since the Bible does not specify how much time passed, either is possible.

The fifth, and perhaps simplest solution, would be to acknowledge the fact that "all" does not always mean exclusively "all."[2] We must use the context to determine its meaning. In the case of Exodus 9:6, it might be best translated that "all manner of livestock of the Egyptians died." In other words, the plague included all kinds of animals, as clarified in the third verse: "on the horses, on the donkeys, on the camels, on the oxen, and on the sheep — a very severe pestilence." This is the approach taken in Coverdale's

---

2. Geisler and Howe wrote, "The term 'all' is often used in a general sense to mean 'the vast majority.' " Norman L. Geisler and Thomas A. Howe, *When Critics Ask: A Popular Handbook on Bible Difficulties* (Wheaton, IL: Victor Books, 1992), p. 73–74.

translation, and the New English Translation includes a footnote with a similar explanation.

The final solution is that not all Egyptians had their livestock in the fields at the time. Many could easily be under shelter or elsewhere, but not in the fields. For the devastation was to take place *in the fields* according to Exodus 9:3. So when the Lord said in verse 6 "and all the livestock of Egypt died," this was in direct reference to that livestock that was present *in the field* that died. This should easily leave sufficient numbers for the later plague which *also* took place in the field (Exodus 9:19, 21, 22, and 25).

Conclusion

All six possibilities have some merit. Perhaps the truth consists of a combination of these views, or there may be another solution not addressed here. In any event, there is no contradiction. God demonstrated He was more powerful than the "gods" of Egypt, and He showed His wrath to the Egyptians and His mercy toward the Hebrews (and perhaps some other subjugated peoples).

War and Peace

⟵ Bodie Hodge ⟶

Is God a God of war or a God of peace?

The "Problem"

Romans 15:33 calls God a God of peace, but Exodus 15:3 calls Him a man of war.

> The LORD is a man of war; the LORD is His name (Exodus 15:3).

> Now the God of peace be with you all. Amen (Romans 15:33).

The Solution

The most basic answer to this supposed contradiction is that both statements are true depending on the time and context. With that in mind, let's examine a couple different ways we can look at this.

First, consider the fact that war is often fought for the purpose of bringing about peace. During World War II, Europe and Asia were engulfed in fighting. Sitting on the sideline was the United States, hoping that this situation would be resolved without our involvement. The United States wanted peace, not war.

On December 7, 1941, Japanese pilots made a surprise attack on Pearl Harbor that launched the United States into war against Japan. That prompted Hitler to declare war on the United States, bringing the country into both fronts. The United States became a nation of war in an effort to be a nation of peace and to help bring peace to the world at that time.

In the same way, God is a God of peace. He created an originally perfect, peaceful world that has been subjected to war only because of mankind's rebellion. Of course, God knew this, had a plan for victory, and offers a time when peace will reign for eternity. However, bringing about this peace often includes the necessity of war.

The context of these passages is also significant. In Exodus, the oppressed Israelites had just been set free from their harsh oppressors, and God fought the battle at the crossing of the Red Sea. The beautiful metaphor in Exodus 15:3, "the LORD is a man of war," reveals the ease, power, and control God had over the situation, doing battle against an oppressing army of Egyptians.

Furthermore, we must consider the recipients of war and the recipients of peace. God has never promised peace to the wicked. In fact, He has stated exactly the opposite. " 'There is no peace,' says the LORD, 'for the wicked' " (Isaiah 48:22). The promises of peace in Romans 15 and elsewhere are given to God's people alone. We should also understand that the peace God gives does not always mean avoidance of trouble, but rather it means we will have God's comfort and assurance while going through difficult times.

Conclusion

In the grand scheme of things, God did not only fight against the Egyptians on behalf of the Israelites, but His ultimate war is against sin and death. Christ conquered these foes on the Cross and now offers peace to those who trust in Him. Paul expounds on this peace in Romans and other epistles (e.g., Romans 5:1, 10:15, 16:20; Philippians 4:7, 9; 1 Thessalonians 5:23; 2 Thessalonians 3:16; Hebrews 13:20). Because they are in Christ, Christians are no longer at war, but rather have peace with God (Ephesians 2:3, 14, 16). A God of peace and a God of war are not in contradiction.

Did Animal Sacrifices Remove Sin?

← Ron Dudek →

Leviticus 4:20–35 seems to teach that animal sacrifices can take away sins, while Hebrews 10:4–11 reveal they did not.

The "Problem"

The Book of Leviticus discusses many of the sacrifices performed by the Levitical priests. In some places, it seems to claim that a particular offering could remove sins.

> And he shall do with the bull as he did with the bull as a sin offering; thus he shall do with it. So the priest shall make atonement for them, and it shall be forgiven them (Leviticus 4:20).

Yet the Book of Hebrews explicitly states that animal blood could not take away sins:

> For it is not possible that the blood of bulls and goats could take away sins (Hebrews 10:4).

The Solution

This is fairly simple to resolve. Nowhere in the Old Testament is it ever claimed that sins were "taken away" (i.e., completely removed) by animal sacrifices. The root of the Hebrew word translated "atonement" in the Old Testament is *kaphar,* which has the idea of "covering," not total removal. This word is also used to refer to how Noah's ark was to be *covered* with pitch:

> Make yourself an ark of gopherwood; make rooms in the ark, and *cover* it inside and outside with pitch (Genesis 6:14, emphasis added).

Tens of thousands of animals were ceremonially slaughtered by Jewish priests for centuries. The spilling of their blood vividly illustrated the deadly seriousness of sin. However, these sacrifices were essentially like a bandage, only acting as a covering for sin. They did not, and could not, remove sin, as Hebrews 10:4 clearly states.

They also pointed forward in time to the only One that could remove sin — Jesus Christ, who shed His precious blood to accomplish that purpose.

> By that will we have been sanctified through the offering of the body of Jesus Christ once for all. And every priest stands ministering daily and offering repeatedly the same sacrifices, which can never take away sins. But this Man, after He had offered one sacrifice for sins forever, sat down at the right hand of God (Hebrews 10:10–12).

The phrase "take away" in verse 11 is translated from the Greek root *periaireō*, which does convey the idea of removal. This is consistent with the use of "atonement" in the Old Testament, as the Levitical sacrifices foreshadowed the final sacrifice of Christ.

Conclusion

Animal sacrifices could only cover sins; they could not remove them. The passage from Hebrews 10 draws a contrast between the animal sacrifices and Christ's sacrifice. The former could never take away sins, but when Christ shed His own blood, it was a once and for all sacrifice that removes sins.

In this alleged contradiction, the solution is found by simply understanding the context and the proper meanings of the words employed within the text.

Do Rabbits Really "Chew the Cud"?

← Tommy Mitchell →

The Bible clearly states that rabbits chew their cud, but simple observation seems to show this isn't true.

The "Problem"

One of the most often cited "contradictions" in the Bible involves the lowly rabbit.[1] Does the Bible actually indicate that rabbits "chew the cud"? And if this is what Scripture says, then isn't it in error?

Two places in the Bible include the hare among animals that chew the cud:

> Among the animals, whatever divides the hoof, having cloven hooves and chewing the cud — that you may eat. Nevertheless these you shall not eat among those that chew the cud or those that have cloven hooves: the camel, because it chews the cud but does not have cloven hooves, is unclean to you; the rock hyrax, because it chews the cud but does not have cloven hooves, is unclean to you; the hare, because it chews the cud but does not have cloven hooves, is unclean to you (Leviticus 11:3–6).

> Nevertheless, of those that chew the cud or have cloven hooves, you shall not eat, such as these: the camel, the hare, and the rock hyrax; for they chew the cud but do not have cloven hooves; they are unclean for you (Deuteronomy 14:7).

In the modern scientific classification system, animals that chew the cud are called ruminants. Cattle, sheep, deer, giraffes, and

---

1. In the modern system of classification, there are differences between hares and rabbits. However, most biblical creationists would consider them to be a part of the same created "kind." For the sake of this discussion, "rabbit" will include both rabbits and hares.

camels[2] are ruminants. Ruminants have four stomach compartments. They swallow their food into one stomach compartment
where food is partially digested. Then the food is regurgitated back
into the mouth, chewed again, and then swallowed into a different
stomach compartment. This process is called rumination.

So is the Bible wrong? After all, rabbits are not ruminants.[3] They
do not have four-compartment stomachs. How can they "chew the
cud"?

The Solution

Obviously, rabbits do not share the digestive anatomy of modern
ruminants. However, to describe rabbits chewing the cud is not
incorrect. Simply stated, it is not reasonable to accuse a 3500-year-
old document of error because it does not adhere to a modern man-
made classification system.

Consider what rabbits do. They engage in an activity called
cecotrophy. Rabbits normally produce two kinds of feces, the more
common hard feces as well as softer fecal pellets called *cecotropes*.
Cecotropes are small pellets of partially digested food that are passed
through the animal but are then reingested. As part of the normal
digestive process, some partially digested food is concentrated in the
cecum where it undergoes a degree of fermentation to form these
cecotropes. They are then covered in mucin and passed through the
anus. The rabbit ingests the cecotropes, which serve as a very important source of nutrition for the animal.

Is this the same as cud? In the final analysis, it is. Cud-chewing
completes the digestion of partially digested food. Why would it be
strange to think that centuries ago the idea of "cud" had a somewhat
broader meaning than a modern definition?

---

2. By some modern classification systems, the camel, the llama, and the alpaca are actually
   "pseudo-ruminants" because they only have three stomach compartments.

3. Although rabbits and horses are not, by definition, ruminants, they are considered "hind-
   gut fermenters." Similar fermentation takes place in the "rumen" compartment of the
   stomach during rumination. Of course, rabbits — but not horses — add reingestion of
   cecotrophs to this process.

But does the rabbit actually *chew* the cud? The Hebrew word translated "chew" is the word *'alah*. With any attempt to translate one language to another, it is understood that there is often more than one meaning for a given word. A cursory glace at any Hebrew lexicon reveals that *'alah* can mean go up, ascend, climb, go up into, out of a place, depart, rise up, cause to ascend, bring up from, among others. Here it carries the implication of moving something from one place to another. So the phrase translated to English as "chew the cud" literally means something on the order of "eats that which is brought forth again."

Also, most reference material on rabbit digestion says that the cecotrope pellet is swallowed whole and found intact in the rabbit stomach. However, experts have observed that rabbits keep the cecotrophe in the mouth for a time before swallowing.[4] So even though the mucin membrane covering the cecotrope is not broken, the rabbit is able to knead it in its mouth before swallowing, possibly to enhance the process of redigestion.

Conclusion

So is the Bible in error here? No it is not. Rabbits re-ingest partially digested foods, as do modern ruminants. They just do so without the aid of multiple stomach compartments.

---

4. R.M. Lockley, *The Private Life of the Rabbit* (Suffolk: The Boydell Press, 1964), p. 105.

Moses — Fit or Feeble?

← Kyle Runge →

Deuteronomy 34 states that Moses was in good health at 120 years old; does Deuteronomy 31 suggest otherwise?

The "Problem"

Some claim that the descriptions of Moses at 120 years old in Deuteronomy 31 and 34 are contradictory.

> Moses was one hundred and twenty years old when he died. His eyes were not dim nor his natural vigor diminished (Deuteronomy 34:7).

> Then Moses went and spoke these words to all Israel. And he said to them: "I am one hundred and twenty years old today. I can no longer go out and come in. Also the Lord has said to me, 'You shall not cross over this Jordan'" (Deuteronomy 31:1–2).

So which is it? Was Moses unable to "go out and come in," or was he hale and hearty at 120? If the latter, how? First let's look at the surrounding context to see if there is anything that might be helpful in solving our riddle. The first verse of chapter 34:1 credits Moses with hiking "from the plains of Moab to Mount Nebo, to the top of Pisgah." This was quite the feat for an old man, let alone one of 120 (at least by today's standards). So it would appear there is a contradiction. After all, how can a man incapable of "going in and coming out" be described as vigorous?

The Solution

This supposed contradiction is a false dilemma. As revealed by the context of Scripture, the phrase "go out and come in" has nothing to do with physical fitness. We can see in Numbers 27 that it was used to describe the leadership given to Moses.

"Let the LORD, the God of the spirits of all flesh, set a man over the congregation, who may *go out before them and go in before them*, who may lead them out and bring them in, that the congregation of the LORD may not be like sheep which have no shepherd" (Numbers 27:16–17, emphasis added).

We can also see this phrase later used by Solomon.

"Now give me wisdom and knowledge, that I *may go out and come in* before this people; for who can judge this great people of Yours?" (2 Chronicles 1:10, emphasis added).

In neither of these cases does the phrase "go out and come in" refer to the physical rigors of life. Rather, it refers to the leading of the people. And so, the picture becomes clear, which is why the context says that the Lord said Moses would not cross over the Jordan with them.

Conclusion

The Israelites were at the border of the Promised Land — a land which Moses could not enter (per the punishment God decreed in Numbers 20). It was time for Joshua to take the reins and lead the people into the inheritance God had promised them. When Moses said he could "no longer go out and come in," he simply meant that God had revoked his right to lead the people.

The question then becomes, how could Moses really be physically fit enough to climb a mountain at 120 years old? Exodus 6 actually explains this rather handily, as it lists the lifespans of Amram (the father of Moses), Kohath (grandfather), and Levi (great-grandfather). According to those records, Amram lived to be 137, Kohath reached 133, and Levi also lived to 137. When this information and all the miraculous events surrounding the life of Moses are taken into account, it actually seems more amazing that he died so young!

Unacceptable Offering?

← Tim Chaffey →

Does God really abhor human sacrifice as stated in Deuteronomy 12:31, or did He accept it in the case of Jephthah (Judges 11)?

The "Problem"

The Bible clearly states that God considers human sacrifice to be an abomination.

> You shall not worship the LORD your God in that way; for every abomination to the LORD which He hates they [the pagan nations around Israel] have done to their gods; for they burn even their sons and daughters in the fire to their gods (Deuteronomy 12:31).

Jeremiah 19:4–5 explains that the Israelites had forsaken God by worshiping idols. Specifically, it is stated that some of them had offered their sons as burnt offerings to Baal. Several passages speak of a ritual condemned by God in which children were made to "pass through the fire to Molech" (Leviticus 18:21). Many scholars believe this referred to the sacrifice of children.

Since God is so clearly opposed to human sacrifice, which is murder (Exodus 20:13), how could He seemingly endorse it in the case of Jephthah, which is recorded in Judges 11? This chapter records that Jephthah was a mighty man who was asked by the elders of Gilead to lead the people in a fight against the Ammonites. Prior to the battle, Jephthah made a vow to the Lord:

> "If you will indeed deliver the people of Ammon into my hands, then it will be that whatever comes out of the doors of my house to meet me, when I return in peace from the people of Ammon, shall surely be the LORD's, and I will offer it up as a burnt offering" (Judges 11:30–31).

Jephthah then advanced against the Ammonites and the Lord delivered them into his hand.

If this was the end of the account, then there would not be a supposed contradiction. However, when Jephthah returned home, his daughter came out of the house to meet him. When he saw her, "he tore his clothes and said, 'Alas, my daughter! You have brought me very low! You are among those who trouble me! For I have given my word to the LORD, and I cannot go back on it" (Judges 11:35).

Obviously, Jephthah expected to see an animal come out of the house upon his return, but that wasn't the case. After granting his daughter two months with her friends to mourn over the fact that she would never marry, the Bible states, "And it was so at the end of two months that she returned to her father, and he carried out his vow with her which he had vowed" (Judges 11:39).

The Solution

This incident immediately raises some red flags. Since God knows all things, including the future, then He knew that Jephthah's daughter would exit the house before any of the animals when Jephthah came home. Consequently, critics have charged that God endorsed this instance of child sacrifice. There are at least two plausible solutions to this difficulty.

First, many people believe Jephthah did not actually sacrifice his daughter as a burnt offering. Instead, they believe that Jephthah gave his daughter to be a lifelong virgin who would serve at Israel's main sanctuary. The text stresses that she was a virgin, so this may be a possibility. If this is the proper interpretation then there is certainly no contradiction. However, this view seems contrary to the straightforward reading of the text.

The second option is to point out that the plain reading of the text indicates Jephthah actually sacrificed her as a burnt offering. After all, he did promise to offer up as a burnt offering the first thing that came out of the doors of his house (Judges 11:31). Then verse 39 states that "he carried out his vow with her which he had vowed."

However, just because God granted him victory does not mean the Lord endorsed Jephthah's vow. So this is enough to show this is no legitimate contradiction. God used Jephthah as a judge to protect the people of Israel against the people of Ammon who were oppressing them. The Bible does not state that God approved of Jephthah's vow. What we can learn is that one should be cautious about making vows.

Consider the alternative. If God did not empower Jephthah to win the battle, then many more Israelites would have been killed, perhaps even Jephthah and the families in places where the Ammonites would overrun. In fact, throughout the period of the Judges, God used certain men, even some ungodly men, to free the Israelites from their oppressors. Prior to this battle, the Bible reveals that Jephthah was part of a group of "worthless men" (Judges 11:3). He is never described as a godly man.[1] So it seems that God would have granted the victory to Jephthah with or without a vow because He was protecting Israel.

This is a classic example of critics turning an inference into an implication. In other words, they have assumed, since God granted victory to Jephthah and the Israelites, that He must have been pleased with the vow and subsequent sacrifice as well. Yet God has often used sinful people and nations to accomplish His will without endorsing their wicked ways. He used the Babylonians to conquer Judah and to lead the people away to Babylon, but He never condoned the pagan religious practices of the Babylonians.

Abraham and Isaac

Critics have also alleged that Genesis 22 contradicts other passages on the subject of child sacrifice. God told Abraham to take Isaac "and go to the land of Moriah, and offer him there as a burnt offering on one of the mountains of which I shall tell you." In an

---

1. Jephthah is listed in Hebrews 11, which is often called the "Faith Hall of Fame," but it is important to notice that he is listed with Gideon, Barak, and Samson (Hebrews 11:32). When they trusted Him, God used these men to win important victories in the Book of Judges, but each of them had serious problems, such as idolatry (Judges 8:27), cowardice (Judges 4:8), and infidelity (Judges 16:1), respectively. So we should not necessarily hold them up as example of godliness.

incredible display of trust, Abraham attempted to carry out God's instructions, but God prevented him from sacrificing Isaac.

> But the Angel of the LORD called to him from heaven and said, "Abraham, Abraham!"
> So he said, "Here I am."
> And He said, "Do not lay your hand on the lad, or do anything to him; for now I know that you fear God, since you have not withheld your son, your only son, from Me" (Genesis 22:11–12).

What was going on here? Did God really want Abraham to sacrifice Isaac as a burnt offering? If so, why did the Lord stop him from doing it? Well, Hebrews 11 answers these questions for us:

> By faith Abraham, when he was *tested*, offered up Isaac, and he who had received the promises offered up his only begotten son, of whom it was said, "In Isaac your seed shall be called," concluding that God was able to raise him up, even from the dead, from which he also received him in a figurative sense (Hebrews 11:17–19, emphasis added).

God gave Abraham an opportunity to display his trust in Him, and he passed with flying colors. Abraham knew that God had already promised that Isaac would have numerous descendants (Genesis 17:19). He reasoned that even if he killed his own son, God would raise him from the dead so that this promise could be fulfilled.

Conclusion

God's Word clearly stands against human sacrifice. Jephthah apparently sacrificed his own daughter in fulfillment of his rash vow. He would have been more Christ-like if he would have been willing to be sacrificed in her place. In the case of Abraham and Isaac, God provided a substitute in the ram that was caught in a thicket (Genesis 22:13). While Abraham demonstrated his incredible trust in God, this account reminds us of something far greater. Roughly 2,000 years after Abraham, God provided the ultimate substitute when He sent *His only Son* to die in our place on the Cross to save us.

Joshua – Malachi

Pillars or Nothing?

← Erik Lutz →

Is the earth immovably set on pillars or hanging on nothing?

The "Problem"

> For the pillars of the earth are the LORD's, and He has set the world upon them (1 Samuel 2:8).

> He stretches out the north over empty space; He hangs the earth on nothing (Job 26:7).

At first glance, these verses appear to contradict each other: how can the earth rest on pillars and at the same time hang on nothing? But remember that a true contradiction would be more like "hangs on nothing" versus "hangs on something" in the same time and same relationship.

In addition, the idea of the earth having "pillars" and "foundations" seems to defy observations of our planet from afar. To some it may even sound vaguely like various pagan beliefs, such as the Hindu idea that the earth is supported on the backs of four elephants that stand on the shell of a gigantic tortoise. But we should not view these biblical statements as myths, because God's Word is truth (John 17:17), and with this there will surely be an easy explanation.

The Solution

The supposed contradiction quickly disappears when we examine the context of each passage and recognize it as figurative language. First Samuel 2:8 was spoken during a prayer by Hannah after she dedicated her son Samuel into the Lord's service. Job spoke the other verse while talking with his friends about man's weakness in light of God's majestic power. This sort of poetic imagery (pillars, foundations, etc.) is commonly used in Scripture to describe how God upholds the world. For example, consider what the Lord said to Job:

> "Where were you when I laid the foundations of the earth? Tell Me, if you have understanding. Who determined its measurements? Surely you know! Or who stretched the line upon it? To what were its foundations fastened? Or who laid its cornerstone[?]" (Job 38:4–6).

We know that the earth does not literally have foundations and a cornerstone like a building; instead, God uses this figurative language to create a mental picture for Job. In the same way, animals do not talk and laugh, yet God also tells Job that the horse "laughs at fear" and "when the trumpet sounds, he says 'Aha!' " (Job 39:22, 25).[1]

This is something we are all familiar with in everyday speech. For example, if someone is not particularly sane, we might say he's "got bats in the belfry," "losing his marbles," "coming unglued," or "vacant upstairs." All of these are obviously not literal statements but rather figures of speech that give a more interesting look at the concept being expressed.

Critics of our ministry often ridicule *Answers in Genesis* because we endorse the historical-grammatical hermeneutic. They claim that we must take everything in the Bible in a wooden literal sense. However, the historical-grammatical hermeneutic recognizes figures of speech are used in everyday language, and we should interpret them as such. When we interpret Scripture, we strive to find the author's intended meaning. Just as we use figurative language today, so also the writers of Scripture often used figures of speech, especially in passages written using poetic language like the examples above.

---

1. Of course, there were instances that were "out of the norm" where animals talked, such as the serpent in Genesis 3, but this was by the hand of Satan, and Balaam's donkey in Numbers 22:28–31 by the hand of the Lord.

God hangs the earth on nothing, but it's not just dangling in space. He has firmly fixed an orbit for our planet and upholds it securely in its proper place in our solar system. So the passage in Job indeed reveals an intriguing truth even with it figurative meaning. Likewise, the meaning of the pillars of the earth is figurative for the power of God who upholds all things by the very word of His power (Hebrews 1:3). The Bible is consistent and there is no contradiction here. Both passages have clear meanings when properly understood and are complementary.

Generational Gaffe?

← Tim Chaffey →

1 Samuel 9:1 states that Kish (Saul's father) was the son of Abiel, but 1 Chronicles states that Kish was the son of Ner . . . so which is it?

The Problem

The Bible seems to present two different lineages for the first king of Israel. Saul's father was named Kish, but when we try to figure out the name of Kish's father, we run into a complication.

First Samuel 9:1 states, "There was a man of Benjamin whose name was Kish the son of Abiel, the son of Zeror, the son of Bechorath, the son of Aphiah, a Benjamite, a mighty man of power." Later in the same book, we are told, "Kish was the father of Saul, and Ner the father of Abner was the son of Abiel" (1 Samuel 14:51). So 1 Samuel presents Saul and Abner as cousins whose fathers (Kish and Ner, respectively) were sons of a man named Abiel.

When we turn to 1 Chronicles 8:33, we find an apparent contradiction. It states, "Ner begot Kish [and] Kish begot Saul." This same wording is repeated in 1 Chronicles 9:39.

So was Saul's grandfather named Abiel or Ner? Furthermore, was Ner Saul's uncle as 1 Samuel implies or was he Saul's grandfather? Is there any way to resolve these difficulties?

The Solution

There are several possible solutions to properly identify Saul's grandfather. However, the Bible does not provide us with a definitive answer, so we should not dogmatically hold to any of these plausible explanations. Yet, since we only need to show why this is not a contradiction, any of these resolutions will suffice.

One possibility is that in the genealogies provided, some of the generations were skipped. In this case, Abiel could have been Saul's grandfather and Ner could have been several generations earlier or vice versa. While this is plausible, it seems unlikely, given that 1 Samuel 9:1 provides us with the names of three ancestors prior to Abiel and Ner is not one of them. Perhaps he was four generations earlier or more.

Another possible solution is the one I think makes the most sense. It is very possible that Abiel and Ner were simply two names for the same person. Several men in Scripture are called by different names (Abram/Abraham, Jacob/Israel, Reuel/Jethro, Gideon/Jerubbaal, Solomon/Jedidiah, Simon/Peter, etc.). In modern times we often go by first and last names, and sometimes even a middle name, to distinguish us from others who might share our name. In a culture where people were given one name at birth another convention seems to have arisen to make distinctions between people of the same name. Often one's personality would lead to the receiving of a second name, sort of like a nickname.

If Abiel and Ner were just two names for the same man then this would solve both of the difficulties mentioned above. First Samuel 14:50 clearly states that Saul's uncle was named Ner and 1 Chronicles asserts that his grandfather's name was also Ner. According to this scenario, Saul's grandfather (Ner, also known as Abiel) named his son Ner.

Further support for this is found in the fact that this son named Ner (who was Saul's Uncle Ner) passed his name to his son Abner ("my father is Ner"). In Hebrew, the name Ner means a "lamp"[1] and Abner means "my father is a lamp."[2] So perhaps Saul's grandfather was originally named Ner, but, perhaps due to godly character, came to be known as Abiel, which means "God is my father."[3]

Since there are so many names of which to keep track, it may be easier to understand this proposed solution by seeing it diagrammed as a family tree.

---

1. James Strong, *The Exhaustive Concordance of the Bible*, electronic ed. (Ontario: Woodside Bible Fellowship, 1996), s.v. #5369.

2. Ibid., s.v. #74.

3. Ibid., s.v. #22.

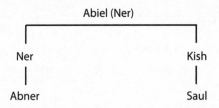

Conclusion

Although we cannot be certain this is the actual solution to the problem, the second option seems to be the most likely scenario. It fits with the common practice of a person going by two names. It also solves the alleged contradiction that one person named Ner was both Saul's uncle and his grandfather. Instead, both his uncle and grandfather shared the same name, just like many people today who are named after their fathers. For example, in my own family, my grandfather, father, brother, and nephew all have the same name. So there are multiple plausible solutions to this alleged contradiction.

A Famine of Three or Seven Years?

← Michael Belknap →

Was David offered three years of famine or seven years of famine?

The "Problem"

After David performed a census of Israel and Judah, the Lord gave David the opportunity to choose one of three possible judgments that would befall his nation. However, at first glance, the two passages that record these options seem to contradict each other.

> So Gad came to David and told him; and he said to him, "Shall seven years of famine come to you in your land? Or shall you flee three months before your enemies, while they pursue you? Or shall there be three days' plague in your land? Now consider and see what answer I should take back to Him who sent me" (2 Samuel 24:13).

> So Gad came to David and said to him, "Thus says the LORD: 'Choose for yourself, either three years of famine, or three months to be defeated by your foes with the sword of your enemies overtaking you, or else for three days the sword of the LORD — the plague in the land, with the angel of the LORD destroying throughout all the territory of Israel.' Now consider what answer I should take back to Him who sent me" (1 Chronicles 21:11–12).

At first glance, it does appear that the above verses contain an inconsistency: one passage offers a choice of three years famine, while the other seemingly offers seven years of famine.

The Solution

Regarding 2 Samuel 24:13, many English translations follow the Septuagint by using "three" in place of "seven." If this were the original reading, then we would have an example of a copyist error. It is possible for copyist errors to have crept into some documents, and since the doctrine of inerrancy only applies to the original manuscripts, such errors would have no impact on this crucial doctrine.

Not surprisingly, some critics of biblical authority present this apparent incongruity as evidence confirming their pre-committed disbelief in the inerrancy and divine inspiration of Scripture. Others cite this to justify their claim that modern copies of the biblical texts insufficiently represent the original manuscripts.

In reality, these accusations of corruption are unwarranted, and there are at least a couple of plausible solutions that do not appeal to a copyist error.

The key lies in understanding the greater context of the account. Let us first consider a verse that precedes the account in 2 Samuel:

> Now there was a famine in the days of David for three years, year after year; and David inquired of the LORD. And the LORD answered, "It is because of Saul and his bloodthirsty house, because he killed the Gibeonites" (2 Samuel 21:1).

Clearly, Israel had already experienced three years of famine before David numbered the people of Israel and Judah — for reasons unrelated to the situation in question. Second Samuel 24:1–7 records the initiation of the census, but we find in verse 8 that "when they had gone through all the land, they came to Jerusalem at the end of nine months and twenty days."

So according to the text, numbering the people was nearly a year-long process, and there is no clear indication that God had suspended the initial three-year famine prior to the events in chapter 24. Now if God had combined three *additional* years of famine (1 Chronicles 21:12) with the three years of *initial* famine, and a possible intervening year while the census was conducted, the resulting overall famine would have totaled about seven years (2 Samuel 24:13).

Some Christians have proposed another solution. They claim that these two passages describe Gad confronting David on two different occasions. According to this view, the "seven year" proposal was initially given four years prior to the "three year" proposal. Thus, the prophet would have confronted David and given him a few years to mull over his decision. During that time, David had repented of his actions so God reduced the time of punishment — something God definitely has the authority to do. A problem with this view is that if God reduced the seven years to three years because of David's repentance, then why didn't He reduce the length of the other options as well? So while this solution may seem less likely, it still provides another reasonable explanation.

Conclusion

The important thing to realize is that regardless of the solution, the result is the same. The accusation of contradiction evaporates — all without declaring the text in error. In conclusion, these Scriptures not only are compatible, but also work together to provide additional details on this particular event.

Balancing the Budget

← Kyle Runge →

Second Samuel and 1 Chronicles seem to claim that David paid different prices to different individuals for the site of the temple.

The "Problem"

The account of David's census of the Israelites is found both at the end of 2 Samuel and in chapter 21 of 1 Chronicles. In each account we are told that the census angered God and that He offered David a choice between three punishments: famine, war, or plague. David chose plague at the hands of the God he knew to be just instead of placing himself at the mercy of wicked men or starvation for his people.

God sent an angel to execute His judgment, and not long after, He sent word to David through a prophet named Gad that he should build an altar to God at a certain place to end the plague. David went up to the threshing floor of the man Gad had specified and bought the man's floor, tools, and oxen, along with the surrounding land.

Here is where the two records appear to disagree. Note the differences in the following passages:

> Then the king said to Araunah, "No, but I will surely buy it from you for a price; nor will I offer burnt offerings to the LORD my God with that which costs me nothing." So David bought the threshing floor and the oxen for fifty shekels of silver (2 Samuel 24:24).

> Then King David said to Ornan, "No, but I will surely buy it for the full price, for I will not take what is yours for the LORD, nor offer burnt offerings with that which costs me nothing." So

David gave Ornan six hundred shekels of gold by weight for the place (1 Chronicles 21:24–25).

So we appear to be faced with not one but two problems: What was the name of the man who owned the land? And, how much did David pay him?

The Solution

In response to the first question, there are at least two strong possibilities.[1] It may be that Ornan also went by the name Araunah, just like many others in that culture.[2] Another plausible solution is that, in the original Hebrew, one of these names is simply a variant spelling of the other. This is suggested in Strong's Lexicon, which identifies Araunah as an "orthographical variation" of Ornan.[3]

As to the second problem, it would seem we have two very different amounts for almost the same purchase. It's nearly impossible to imagine either David or the owner of the threshing floor confusing 50 shekels of silver (~$1,067 today) with 600 of gold (~$594,198), and so it would appear as if those believing the Bible to be untrustworthy were vindicated. After all, if such a gross error has been made in mere record-keeping, then what hope is there for the reliability of more complicated passages? If such an oversight is excusable, then aren't reports of miracles hopelessly suspect? Sadly, as fallen human beings these are often our first thoughts as we repeat the mistake of the Jewish people in believing God to be "altogether like [us]" (Psalm 50:21). If we instead allow Scripture to inform our thoughts and look back at the overall account more closely, we

---

1. There may be a third option but I would remain tentative on it. That solution would be that these are two different people (both Jebusites living in the same area, being descendants of Jebuseus, the Canaanite, who founded Jerusalem) with two different purchases that were both involved in the sacrifices to end the plague. One the gents came out to meet David, the other remained threshing before he came out. Two different sets of oxen and two different (perhaps adjoining properties) and it is possible that David needed both for the large Temple site as well enough oxen to provide the proper sacrifice called for by God.

2. See section on "Generational Gaffe," for discussion of this common practice.

3. James Strong, *The Exhaustive Concordance of the Bible*, electronic ed. (Ontario: Woodside Bible Fellowship, 1996). #771 ('Ornan).

should notice that in both records David is offered the entire portion for free but refuses to accept it. David, in recognizing his need for atonement before God, declares that he will not offer a sacrifice that has, in his words, "cost him nothing."

So, does this mean that 1 Chronicles has the correct exchange while 2 Samuel is in error? Not at all! If we read just a little further in the Bible, we find the resolution to our alleged conflict in David's need to pay a fair price. First Chronicles 22:1 explains that David bought the land surrounding the threshing floor with the intention of ultimately building the temple there, which his son Solomon later did.

Second Chronicles 3:3–4 gives us a hint at the minimum area of the land David purchased. The foundation of the temple was 60 cubits by 20 cubits, and the vestibule in front of it added an additional 10 cubits to the length. Three tiers of chambers were added to the two sides and back of the temple, the widest of which was seven cubits. This gives us the total dimensions for the temple at about 77 by 34 cubits.

The Bible specifically mentions that the dimensions were in cubits "by the former measure," which makes them each roughly 20.5 inches. This would make the layout of the completed temple about 131.5 feet by 58 feet. When the Bronze Sea, the ten smaller carts for washing, and the outer altar are included, the total footprint grows to approximately 10,000 square feet.

So then, with this new information it becomes clear that 600 shekels of gold were paid for the lands surrounding the threshing floor, a large enough area for at least Solomon's later temple. The purchased land may have been large enough to encompass Solomon's future palace and several other buildings mentioned in 1 Kings 7–8 (e.g., the House of the Forest of Lebanon, which alone was nearly twice the size of the temple).

Whatever the square footage of the final plot of land, we can be certain David paid at least a fair price, if not a premium one. The 50 shekels of silver were paid for the oxen, equipment, and the threshing floor itself (with which David made an offering to the Lord), bringing the final total Ornan (Araunah) received to 600 shekels of gold *and* 50 of silver, almost $600,000 in today's currency. Clearly, David got his wish, since his sacrifice to God for the plague cost him much more than "nothing" — a good price even for a king.

Conclusion

Araunah and Ornan are variations of the same name, and they refer to the same person. The account found in 2 Samuel 24 records only David's purchase of the threshing floor and oxen. On the other hand, the account in 1 Chronicles 21 records a higher price for the full purchase, including the surrounding land.

Longevity or Countdown?

⭠ David Chakranarayan ⭢

How long did God say people will live after Noah?

The "Problem"

The Bible seems to contradict itself in Genesis and Psalms when speaking about the expected life spans of individuals.

> And the LORD said, "My Spirit shall not strive with man forever, for he is indeed flesh; yet his days shall be one hundred and twenty years" (Genesis 6:3).

> The days of our lives are seventy years; and if by reason of strength they are eighty years, yet their boast is only labor and sorrow; for it is soon cut off, and we fly away (Psalm 90:10).

The supposed contradiction in these two verses has to do with the length of a person's life on earth, namely his or her total years of existence. The passage in Genesis seems to indicate that a human being will not be able to live beyond 120 years of age, but the passage in Psalms seems to limit the time span to 80 years.

The Solution

In the context of Genesis 6:3, Moses wrote about the tremendous evil in the world during the time of Noah. He highlighted the sinfulness of the people in very strong terms.

> Then the LORD saw that the wickedness of man was great in the earth, and that every intent of the thoughts of his heart was only evil continually. And the LORD was sorry that He had made man on the earth, and He was grieved in His heart. So the LORD said, "I will destroy man whom I have created from the face of the earth, man and beast, creeping thing and birds of the air, for I am sorry that I have made them" (Genesis 6:5–8).

The severity of the people's sin would result in global judgment from God. Because of their depravity, God destroyed every human being and even the animals. In this context, we can see that Genesis 6:3 does not deal with the length of time a human will live. Rather, it indicates the longsuffering nature of God in the midst of His wrath. He was allowing even the most evil people of Noah's time 120 years to repent of their sin before He would judge them with a global Flood. Genesis 6:8 says, "But Noah found grace in the eyes of the LORD." During this time, Noah was a preacher of righteousness, and he also built an ark for his family and himself.

In the context of Psalm 90:10, Moses pleaded for God's mercy on human beings who live in a sin-cursed world. He reflected on the eternal attributes of God and contrasted them with the finite existence of man. Man, because of sin and disobedience, brought on himself wrath and judgment from a holy God.

> For we have been consumed by Your anger, and by Your wrath we are terrified. You have set our iniquities before You, our secret sins in the light of Your countenance (Psalm 90:7–8).

Moses informed us that the length of a man's life averages out to between 70 and 80 years on earth (Psalm 90:10), even though Moses himself far exceeded this. Due to this time span, Moses said, "So teach us to number our days, that we may gain a heart of wisdom" (Psalm 90:12). We are to live the remainder of our days in wisdom and holiness with the chief aim of pleasing God with our lives.

Conclusion

The Genesis passage deals with God's longsuffering and the length of time He is willing to allow people to repent. The Psalm deals with finite humans who are in need of God's mercy. Upon careful examination, we can conclude that these passages both give us important insight into the existence of human beings and the judgment that each human must face when his or her time on earth has concluded. Whether a human being lives to be 80 or 120, his or her time on earth is very brief when seen from God's perspective.

> For a thousand years in Your sight are like yesterday when it is past, and like a watch in the night. You carry them away like a flood; they are like a sleep. In the morning they are like grass which grows up: in the morning it flourishes and grows up; in the evening it is cut down and withers (Psalm 90:4–6).

> For what is your life? It is even a vapor that appears for a little time and then vanishes away (James 4:14).

The brevity of our life should cause us to examine our spiritual condition to see whether we are prepared to spend eternity in heaven with Jesus or eternal separation from Him in hell.

When Were the Stars Created?

← David Wright →

Were the stars created before or after the creation of the earth?

The "Problem"

It's clear the Bible's historical account of creation can in no way be meshed with the secular story about the big bang. The order in which the events happen just don't line up. For example, the Bible records God creating the stars after He created the earth, water, land, and plants; whereas big-bang proponents claim that the stars came first, then the earth, then the land, then the seas, and then plants. So skeptics, in order to justify their false beliefs, try to discredit the Bible in any way they can. If they can find a contradiction, then they can disprove the account of creation and so better justify their beliefs.

One such "contradiction" they try to assert has to do with *when* the stars were created. Here are the passages involved.

> Then God made two great lights: the greater light to rule the day, and the lesser light to rule the night. He made the stars also. God set them in the firmament of the heavens to give light on the earth, and to rule over the day and over the night, and to divide the light from the darkness. And God saw that it was good. So the evening and the morning were the fourth day (Genesis 1:16–19).

> Where were you when I laid the foundations of the earth? Tell Me, if you have understanding. Who determined its measurements? Surely you know! Or who stretched the line upon it? To what were its foundations fastened? Or who laid its cornerstone,

when the morning stars sang together, and all the sons of God shouted for joy? (Job 38:4–7).

When interpreted incorrectly one might assume that Job 38 is implying the stars were there when the earth was created. This would of course contradict the Genesis account.

The Solution

However, a simple explanation exists. The stars referred to in Job are not literally stars. These passages in Job are poetic in nature, meaning that words are often used in a figurative sense. When we look at Job 38 these stars *are singing* and also called "sons of God" who can *shout with joy*.

Clearly, these are not literal stars like those created on day 4 of Genesis 1. Scripture sometimes uses stars as a metaphorical reference for angels or people. For example, see the following passages:

> They fought from the heavens; the stars from their courses fought against Sisera (Judges 5:20).

> And it grew up to the host of heaven; and it cast down some of the host and some of the stars to the ground, and trampled them (Daniel 8:10).

> Raging waves of the sea, foaming up their own shame; wandering stars for whom is reserved the blackness of darkness forever (Jude 1:13).

> The mystery of the seven stars which you saw in My right hand, and the seven golden lampstands: The seven stars are the angels of the seven churches, and the seven lampstands which you saw are the seven churches (Revelation 1:20).

> His tail drew a third of the stars of heaven and threw them to the earth. And the dragon stood before the woman who was ready to give birth, to devour her Child as soon as it was born (Revelation 12:4).

Conclusion

These singing stars mentioned in Job were not the literal stars in the sky. They were angelic beings who witnessed the creation. The literal historical account states that the literal stars were created on day 4. This supposed contradiction disappears like faint starlight when the sun comes up.

Matthew
~John

Did Jesus Go Up or Down the Mountain?

⟐ Tim Chaffey ⟐

Did Jesus go up or down the mountain to deliver the Sermon on the Mount?

The "Problem"

The Gospel of Matthew indicates Jesus "went up on a mountain" before preaching the famous Sermon on the Mount. Meanwhile, the gospel of Luke reveals that Jesus "came down" before delivering this message. Furthermore, Matthew showed that Jesus "was seated" before teaching while Luke stated that Jesus "stood on a level place." How can both accounts possibly be accurate? Let's take a look at the two passages and then find out why these are not contradictions.

> And seeing the multitudes, He *went up on a mountain*, and when He *was seated* His disciples came to Him. Then He opened His mouth and taught them, saying: "Blessed are the poor in spirit, for theirs is the kingdom of heaven" (Matthew 5:1–3, emphasis added).

> Now it came to pass in those days that He went out to the mountain to pray, and continued all night in prayer to God. And when it was day, He called His disciples to Himself. . . . And He *came down with them* and *stood on a level place* with a crowd of His disciples and a great multitude of people from all Judea and Jerusalem. . . . Then He lifted up His eyes toward His disciples, and said: Blessed are you poor, for yours is the kingdom of God (Luke 6:12–20, emphasis added).

Possible Solutions

There are at least two possible solutions to these apparent contradictions. One possible solution to each of the difficulties is that Matthew and Luke recorded two separate events. Though an option, this does not seem to be the best answer, since both gospels record similar events before and after the Sermon. They also show that it took place in the same geographical area and was delivered to the same group of people. So although this scenario is possible, it seems unlikely that these are separate accounts of two different, yet similar sermons.

Let's look at the location of this sermon. The Gospel of Matthew provides a brief summary of the Lord's activities in that region during the weeks and perhaps months leading up to the message. Following that summary, Matthew simply stated that Jesus "went up on a mountain." On the other hand, Luke provided specific details about Christ's activities the night before the Sermon on the Mount. "He went out to the mountain to pray, and continued all night in prayer to God" (Luke 6:12). In the morning Jesus called 12 of His followers and came down the mountain to preach.

The simple answer is that Matthew summarized the Lord's movements prior to the message. He did not specifically mention that Jesus went out to the mountain and prayed throughout the night before teaching. So Matthew skipped those details and just mentioned that Jesus went up the mountain and delivered the Sermon on the Mount. If Jesus went higher up the mountain to pray the night before, then Matthew's and Luke's accounts are in agreement. Jesus went up the mountain to pray and came back down some of the way to a level place on the mountain before delivering the Sermon on the Mount.

So was Jesus standing or sitting as He preached? It is possible He did both. Matthew states that Jesus sat down and then started teaching. This was the common practice among Jews of the day. Teachers would stand when reading Scripture, but they sat during their teaching, just as Jesus did in the synagogue in Nazareth (Luke 4:16–21).

Once again, Luke provides more details leading up to the Sermon, whereas Matthew records more of the message itself. Luke shows that Jesus "stood on a level place" and healed all the people who came to Him.

> And He came down with them and stood on a level place with a crowd of His disciples and a great multitude of people from all Judea and Jerusalem, and from the seacoast of Tyre and Sidon, who came to hear Him and be healed of their diseases, as well as those who were tormented with unclean spirits. And they were healed. And the whole multitude sought to touch Him, for power went out from Him and healed them all (Luke 6:17–19).

There are at least two obvious solutions to this sitting or standing dilemma. First, Jesus sat at the beginning of the Sermon but then stood and moved about during the course of the message. A better solution is found by closely looking at the text. Jesus stood while healing the multitude, and this may have taken several hours. Then, after healing people, He sat down and delivered the Sermon on the Mount.

Conclusion

Both of these alleged contradictions are easily explained upon closer examination of the text, but issues like this highlight an important point. Many skeptics have accused the New Testament writers, especially Matthew, Mark, and Luke, of being in collusion (i.e., they got together to make sure they got their stories straight.). However, if these writers were in collusion, they would have used similar (or identical) wording in each of these accounts. The fact that these apparent disagreements exist demonstrate that these men were largely independent of each other and were not in collusion.[1] They were guided by the Holy Spirit to write the words they used, and when we look closely at the text, we see that the accounts can be harmonized without much difficulty.

---

1. Most modern biblical scholars believe Mark was written first, and that Matthew and Luke had access to this book as they wrote. This may be true, but it still would not prove collusion since Matthew and Luke wrote independently of each other.

Did Jesus Contradict Himself by Calling People Fools?

⟵ Jeremy Ham ⟶

Is it a contradiction or a matter of context?

The "Problem"

Jesus proclaimed that "whoever says, 'You fool!' shall be in danger of hell fire" (Matthew 5:22). However, there are instances throughout Scripture where people are called fools. For example, David wrote, "The fool has said in his heart, 'There is no God' " (Psalm 14:1). Paul told the Galatians they were foolish (Galatians 3:1). Jesus even said the Pharisees and scribes were fools in Matthew 23:17.

So does the Lord's claim in Matthew 5:22 contradict these other passages where people are actually called fools?

The Solution

When studying Scripture, one of the first principles to keep in mind is the context. Therefore, let us consider the entire context of what Jesus said while considering this alleged contradiction.

> "You have heard that it was said to those of old, 'You shall not murder; and whoever murders will be liable to judgment.' But I say to you that everyone who is angry with his brother will be liable to judgment; whoever insults his brother will be liable to the council; and whoever says, 'You fool!' will be liable to the hell of fire" (Matthew 5:21–22, ESV).

Jesus referred to the generally understood fact that murderers will be judged; however, He revealed the deeper issue by saying that not just murderers but anyone who "is angry with his brother . . . shall be in danger of the judgment." Furthermore, Christ continued by mentioning that those who insult their brother or call their brother a fool would be held liable for those words.

Jesus did not focus just on an individual's actions such as murder, but also on the heart and attitude behind those actions. A heart full of anger toward someone can lead to insults, name calling, and even murder. In other words, murder is not the only symptom of a corrupted heart, which is the main point Jesus made — and this is expected in a sin-cursed world where people are in constant sin (Romans 3:23).

Does this mean that calling people foolish is *always* wrong? Jesus emphasized the fact that not just murderers will be judged by saying that those who call people fools will also be judged. He demonstrated that sin is an issue of the heart rather than just the actions.

If you were to study each biblical example where God calls someone a fool, you will find a righteous reason behind it. When Jesus called the Pharisees and scribes fools in Matthew 23:17, He explained that they were satisfying themselves instead of giving glory to God. They glorified the gold in the temple rather than the temple of God that housed the gold, which is foolish.

Also, keep in mind that Jesus is the Judge and the Lawgiver with perfect knowledge, so He is able to do what humanity cannot do (James 4:11–12). And in everything, we must make sure we are basing our actions and words on the principles of Scripture, and if we are to judge others, we judge righteously from God's Word (John 7:24).

Conclusion

Matthew 5:21–22 serves as a reminder for us to "abstain from every form of evil" (1 Thessalonians 5:22), which includes issues of the heart and not just evil deeds. When we understand the words of Jesus in their full context, there is clearly no contradiction. When we take one statement out of context in an attempt to prove an unfounded idea, we fail to interpret God's Word correctly.

Should Christians Pray in Public or Not?

← Jeremy Ham →

Why did Paul encourage Christians to pray everywhere,
but Jesus said to pray in secret?

The "Problem"

A couple passages in Scripture regarding prayer have been cited as a contradiction. Here are the verses in question:

> I desire therefore that the men pray everywhere, lifting up holy hands, without wrath and doubting (1 Timothy 2:8).

> And when you pray, you shall not be like the hypocrites. For they love to pray standing in the synagogues and on the corners of the streets, that they may be seen by men. Assuredly, I say to you, they have their reward. But you, when you pray, go into your room, and when you have shut your door, pray to your Father who is in the secret place; and your Father who sees in secret will reward you openly. And when you pray, do not use vain repetitions as the heathen do. For they think that they will be heard for their many words. Therefore do not be like them. For your Father knows the things you have need of before you ask Him (Matthew 6:5–8).

Does the passage in Matthew command we should not pray in public whereas the passage in 1 Timothy exhorts us to pray everywhere? If one were to quickly read over these passages without further study, I could see why one would come to this conclusion. When reading the Bible, closely studying God's Word is necessary to gain a proper understanding. This can be as simple as prayerfully reading Scripture while thinking about what the passage means.

Upon a closer reading and study, we will find these verses do not contradict each other at all.

The Solution

First, we will take an in-depth look at 1 Timothy 2:8. In order to better understand this verse, we should start in the Old Testament.

Psalm 141:2 discusses the offering up of evening prayers, which was a custom among Israelites. Hezekiah prayed from what he thought was his deathbed, and the Lord heard his prayer and healed him (2 Kings 20:1–5). Many Jews, like Daniel in Babylon, prayed multiple times a day (Daniel 6:10; 9:3, 23).

However, by the time of Christ's ministry, some Israelites believed that God could only be worshiped (or prayed to) in Jerusalem. Yet Jesus corrected this type of thinking when speaking with the woman at the well.

> [The woman said,] "Our fathers worshiped on this mountain, and you Jews say that in Jerusalem is the place where one ought to worship."
>
> Jesus said to her, "Woman, believe Me, the hour is coming when you will neither on this mountain, nor in Jerusalem, worship the Father. You worship what you do not know; we know what we worship, for salvation is of the Jews. But the hour is coming, and now is, when the true worshipers will worship the Father in spirit and truth; for the Father is seeking such to worship Him. God is Spirit, and those who worship Him must worship in spirit and truth" (John 4:20–24).

Furthermore, in 1 Timothy 2:8, Paul's desire for men to pray everywhere may have been in response to the idea that the Temple was the only place to worship God. Since Jesus died on the Cross and was raised up, the Holy Spirit now lives in each and every believer. We are now the temple of God (2 Corinthians 6:16) and can pray anywhere with the help of the Holy Spirit (Ephesians 6:18; Romans 8:26). Praying in every place fulfills the words of Christ in John 4.

In Matthew 6:5–8, Jesus taught His disciples about prayer in light of a general principle set forth later in the chapter:

> Do not lay up for yourselves treasures on earth, where moth and rust destroy and where thieves break in and steal; but lay up for yourselves treasures in heaven, where neither moth nor rust destroys and where thieves do not break in and steal (Matthew 6:19–20).

We are not to do things for earthly rewards or treasures — getting immediate results from our actions. Instead, we should do things for Christ and lay up treasures in heaven. We may not get results right away, but everything good done for Christ will eventually be rewarded. Should we be satisfied with earthly rewards, or should we desire rewards in heaven for the cause of Christ?

Now let us apply this principle to what Jesus said about prayer. Should we pray to be seen and praised by people who will be amazed at how "spiritual" we sound? Or should we pray to praise God and let our requests be known? Obviously, praying for the sake of being seen by others focuses on earthly rewards.

Matthew 6:5–8 has nothing to do with whether we should pray in public or not. This passage is related to the *reason* we are praying. When Jesus contrasted praying publicly versus praying privately, He showed how we should *not* be selfish but selfless. We should be praying selflessly and glorifying God for His many blessings — while laying up treasures in heaven.

Conclusion

Prayer is a vital aspect of Christian living. We are to "Rejoice always, pray without ceasing, in everything give thanks; for this is the will of God in Christ Jesus for you" (1 Thessalonians 5:16–18). We should work toward a continual state of prayer unto God — praying constantly and always being mentally prepared to pray. Furthermore, we should "Be anxious for nothing, but in everything by prayer and supplication, with thanksgiving, let your requests be made known to God" (Philippians 4:6). We rely upon God to meet all our needs. We have no reason to worry when we have a God who cares about His people.

We can, indeed, pray everywhere, as long as we are praying for the right reasons. Praying for prideful reasons only receives earthly rewards — so there is no contradiction here. In everything we do, our focus should be on Christ, not ourselves. Jesus Christ has done so much for us, and the proper response for the gift of salvation is to show our love to Him and put Him first in our lives. As an added benefit, focusing on Christ will lay up treasures in heaven.

Following the biblical example and looking toward heavenly things is worth so much more than earthly rewards. Sadly, many believe in the exact opposite, and we should pray they might receive the Lord Jesus Christ as their Savior. Also, we should thank God for what He has given us in Jesus Christ.

A Case of Mistaken Identity

← John Bartlett Jr. →

Was John the Baptist Elijah or not?

The "Problem"

Based on Malachi 4:5, the scribes in Christ's day taught that Elijah would return before the coming of the Messiah. Some people openly asked if John the Baptist was Elijah, a proposition he flatly denied. However, Jesus seemed to imply that John was Elijah. Who was right? The following verses are relevant to the proposed contradiction.

> For all the prophets and the law prophesied until John. And if you are willing to receive it, he is Elijah who is to come (Matthew 11:13–14).

> And His disciples asked Him, saying, "Why then do the scribes say that Elijah must come first?"
> Jesus answered and said to them, "Indeed, Elijah is coming first and will restore all things. But I say to you that Elijah has come already, and they did not know him but did to him whatever they wished. Likewise the Son of Man is also about to suffer at their hands." Then the disciples understood that He spoke to them of John the Baptist (Matthew 17:10–13).

> Now this is the testimony of John, when the Jews sent priests and Levites from Jerusalem to ask him, "Who are you?"
> He confessed, and did not deny, but confessed, "I am not the Christ."
> And they asked him, "What then? Are you Elijah?"
> He said, "I am not."
> "Are you the Prophet?"
> And he answered, "No" (John 1:19–21).

The Solution

The skeptics have asked, "Who was lying: John the Baptist or Jesus?" The answer is that neither of them lied.

The problem with many proposed contradictions is that they are either misquoted or quoted out of their context. The incorrect use of quotes, especially when done to raise alleged contradictions, can easily lead the undiscerning Christian astray. However, like most other "contradictions," a closer look at the context reveals the heart of the problem.

The account of John the Baptist starts in the Book of Luke when Gabriel, an angel of the Lord, appears to Zacharias concerning his coming son. Gabriel told Zacharias:

> "Do not be afraid, Zacharias, for your prayer is heard; and your wife Elizabeth will bear you a son, and you shall call his name John. . . . And he will turn many of the children of Israel to the Lord their God. *He will also go before Him in the spirit and power of Elijah, 'to turn the hearts of the fathers to the children'* " (Luke 1:13, 16–17, emphasis added).

It was foretold that the spirit of Elijah would come on John the Baptist. This was not the first time the spirit of Elijah had come upon someone. The second chapter of 2 Kings records the final conversation between Elijah and Elisha, just before Elijah was taken up into heaven by a whirlwind.

> Elisha said, "Please let a double portion of your spirit be upon me."
>
> So [Elijah] said, "You have asked a hard thing. Nevertheless, if you see me when I am taken from you, it shall be so for you; but if not, it shall not be so." Then it happened, as they continued on and talked, that suddenly a chariot of fire appeared with horses of fire, and separated the two of them; and Elijah went up by a whirlwind into heaven.
>
> And Elisha saw it, and he cried out, "My father, my father, the chariot of Israel and its horsemen!" So he saw him no more. (2 Kings 2:9–12)

Verse 15 states, "Now when the sons of the prophets who were at Jericho saw him [Elisha] opposite them, they said, 'The spirit of Elijah rests on Elisha'" (ESV).

Looking carefully at the words in each passage, it is clear that John received the spirit of Elijah in much the same sense that Elisha had. In other words, John and Elisha were *not reincarnations* of Elijah, but they did resemble Elijah *in spirit*.

The scribes asked John if he was Elijah because they apparently expected Elijah to appear before the coming of the Messiah. This expectation was likely based on the last two verses of the Old Testament, in which God stated, "Behold, I will send you Elijah the prophet before the coming of the great and dreadful day of the LORD. And he will turn the hearts of the fathers to the children, and the hearts of the children to their fathers, lest I come and strike the earth with a curse" (Malachi 4:5–6). John responded by directing their attention to his role of preparing the way for the Redeemer as "The voice of one crying in the wilderness" (see Isaiah 40:3; cf. John 1:23).

After understanding the context for the John 1:19–21 passage, it is important to take a look at the Matthew passages to understand why Jesus called John the Baptist the "Elijah who is to come" (Matthew 11:14). Jesus knew, just like John had, that many in the crowd were searching for an appearance of Elijah in the flesh. "For all the Prophets and the Law prophesied until John, and if you are willing to accept it, he is Elijah who is to come" (Matthew 11:13–14, ESV). So by saying, "if you are willing to accept it," He knew that some would not accept the fact that John was a fulfillment of their expectations about the coming Elijah since he had the spirit of Elijah.[1]

Later in Matthew 17, James, John, and Peter asked Jesus about Elijah's coming. They had just seen the transfigured Jesus talking

---

1. This particular subject can get into eschatological issues. For example, some Christians believe that Elijah will actually return prior to Christ's return as one of the two witnesses mentioned in Revelation 11. As such, they would view John the Baptist as a partial fulfillment of the Malachi prophecy. Other believers disagree with this notion and have the witnesses as the Law and prophets (e.g., Romans 3:21, Nehemiah 9:26, etc.). This article should not be viewed as adopting one position over another, as Answers in Genesis does not take a position on the end times other than to believe that Jesus will physically return to earth someday.

with Moses and Elijah, and they asked Him why the scribes claimed that "Elijah must come first" (Matthew 17:10).

> Jesus answered and said to them, "Indeed, Elijah is coming first and will restore all things. But I say to you that Elijah has come already, and they did not know him but did to him whatever they wished. Likewise the Son of Man is also about to suffer at their hands." Then the disciples understood that He spoke to them of John the Baptist (Matthew 17:11–13).

Even though Jesus had already talked about John the Baptist to His disciples (see Matthew 11), He took time to reiterate that John the Baptist was a fulfillment of the coming Elijah.

Conclusion

Although John the Baptist denied those who wondered if he was Elijah in the flesh, Jesus affirmed that John the Baptist had come in the spirit of Elijah. John and Matthew are not in opposition to one another but are perfectly consistent. You can be greatly encouraged that the Word of God stands true. If you are willing to see it, Scripture is always ready to defend itself.

Act Like a Child

← Frost Smith →

Why does the Bible say to be like a child, but then to put away childish things?

The "Problem"

Jesus told His followers that they were supposed to become like little children, yet Paul told his readers to stop acting like children.

> Then Jesus called a little child to Him, set him in the midst of them, and said, "Assuredly, I say to you, unless you are converted and become as little children, you will by no means enter the kingdom of heaven" (Matthew 18:2–3).

> But Jesus said, "Let the little children come to Me, and do not forbid them; for of such is the kingdom of heaven" (Matthew 19:14).

> When I was a child, I spoke as a child, I understood as a child, I thought as a child; but when I became a man, I put away childish things (1 Corinthians 13:11).

How can these seemingly contradictory passages be resolved?

The Solution

As I bathed my baby recently, it occurred to me how heedless she was of her state of undress and total dependence. She had complete trust in me and in my care for her that transcended any concern she could have about her vulnerable state. This reminded me of Adam and Eve in the Garden of Eden and how they were naked and not ashamed (Genesis 2:25) before God, until they ate of the tree of the knowledge of good and evil (Genesis 3). This is the heart of what the Lord meant when He said that unless they become like little children, they will not enter the Kingdom of Heaven.

How much more would God be glorified in our lives if we were as trusting and dependent on Him as my baby daughter is on me? We should go to Him for all our needs, knowing He doesn't look on the outward man (1 Samuel 16:7), but on the heart — and He can even give us a new heart (Ezekiel 36:26).

But then, what about verses that make statements like, "When I was a child, I spoke as a child, I understood as a child, I thought as a child; but when I became a man, I put away childish things" (1 Corinthians 13:11)?

A few ideas need to be distinguished. There is *being* like a child, *acting* like a child, and *understanding* as a child. As we've seen, being like a child is a good thing in proper context. But what does it mean to act like a child? I've thought about this many times, and the conclusion I've come to is that children wear their emotions for everyone to see — good or bad (often bad).

As adults, we learn instead to hide how we feel, or at least the full extent of our feelings. Do we still want to have attention paid to us, to have the best, and to be first? We would be lying to say otherwise, but we learn to control ourselves and allow others to benefit over us on occasion. To demonstrate: you are at a buffet and the person in front of you takes a large portion of the item you were going to get, leaving little or none for you. You probably would get annoyed. That person was selfish, inconsiderate, and, well, childish — and your inward response probably was childish, too. That is one reason why many buffets have a rule that parents must accompany children.

So children are sinners, but babies and toddlers often have a sort of honesty about them — they've not yet become skilled in deceiving others about how they really feel or what they really want. Childish actions reveal the sinful nature we inherit through Adam. *Acting* like a child, then, is not desirable, yet *being* like a child (in the sense of trusting) is.

It's pretty clear that *understanding* like a child would be a bad thing for an adult. There are many complexities to life that take time and age to comprehend — not just physics and mathematics, but also the wisdom to deal with this fallen world. First Corinthians 14:20 hits the nail on the head: "Brethren, do not be children *in understanding*; however, in malice be babes, but in understanding be mature" (emphasis mine).

So in our "outward" relationships to God our Father and to others, we are to be childlike (trusting and honest; not malicious), but not in our understanding (naive). Regarding what we take "in" from the world, we need to be wise, not carried off or tricked by others (Colossians 2:8). Note that this wariness is necessitated by the fallen state of men, who desire to deceive. Ephesians 4:14 says "that we should no longer be children, tossed to and fro and carried about with every wind of doctrine, by the trickery of men, in the cunning craftiness of deceitful plotting." This wariness is something that is generally lacking in children, as well as in unwise adults (a fact that is sadly taken advantage of by many).

Conclusion

So, are we to be childlike? Well, yes and no — depending on the context. Just as Jesus said in Matthew 10:16, "Therefore be as shrewd as snakes and as innocent as doves" (NIV). Is there a conflict there? Absolutely not! Be loving and dependent on your heavenly Father, whom you can trust, but be wary of the things of this world, where trust can be a dangerous thing.

How, then, do we gain understanding? Scripture tells us that the beginning of wisdom is the fear of the Lord (Psalm 111:10) and that we should hide God's Word in our heart so we might not sin against Him (Psalm 119:11). Our knowledge of God through His Word will aid us in growing spiritually and resisting the deceit and dangers of this world — from others and even from our own deceitful hearts (Jeremiah 17:9). Regardless, these verses are not in contradiction.

Mother Knows Best

← David Wright →

The Book of Matthew states that the mother of James and John asked Jesus for a special privilege, while the Book of Mark declares that James and John actually asked for this honor.

The "Problem"

Who asked Jesus for seats to his right and left?

> Then the mother of Zebedee's sons came to Him with her sons, kneeling down and asking something from Him. And He said to her, "What do you wish?" She said to Him, "Grant that these two sons of mine may sit, one on Your right hand and the other on the left, in Your kingdom" (Matthew 20:20–21).

> Then James and John, the sons of Zebedee, came to Him, saying, "Teacher, we want You to do for us whatever we ask." And He said to them, "What do you want Me to do for you?" They said to Him, "Grant us that we may sit, one on Your right hand and the other on Your left, in Your glory" (Mark 10:35–37).

The Solution

There are a couple of rather simple explanations for this dilemma. It is often said that the Gospel accounts are not contradictory, but complementary.

One possibility is that Mark recorded one instance where James and John approached Jesus and requested of Him, "Grant us that we may sit, one on Your right hand and the other on Your left, in Your glory." In Mark 10:40 Jesus told them, "to sit on My right hand and on My left is not Mine to give, but it is for those for whom it is prepared."

Slightly disappointed and probably not understanding what Jesus was talking about, James and John returned to their mom and told her about His response. Then perhaps she thought, *Maybe He will listen to me*, or maybe they asked her to ask for them. Surely Jesus could not turn down someone's sweet mother, especially considering the possibility that she was also the Lord's aunt.[1] And so Matthew recorded another encounter.

Later, James and John returned with their mother, and she approached Jesus herself with the request, "Grant that these two sons of mine may sit, one on Your right hand and the other on the left, in Your kingdom" (Matthew 20:21). Once again, in Matthew 20:23 Jesus replied, "To sit on My right hand and on My left is not Mine to give, but it is for those for whom it is prepared by My Father."

Another possibility is that Matthew and Mark recorded the same event but focused on different individuals. In other words, James and John came with their mother and asked Jesus about sitting with Him in His kingdom. It may be that all three of them asked the question, or that they asked as a group.

Matthew states that James and John came to Jesus with their mother. When Jesus asked, "What do you wish?" she asked for her sons to be granted the honor of sitting at the Lord's side in His kingdom (Matthew 20:21).

In Mark, we are told that James and John came to Jesus and asked for this honor. He does not mention the appearance of their mother, but this doesn't mean she wasn't there. Mark may have simply focused on the audacity of the two brothers in asking Jesus this question. After all, the rest of the disciples were quite perturbed that the brothers asked this question.

The fact that the discussion between Jesus and the two brothers following the initial question is virtually identical in both books

---

1. By comparing Matthew 4:21; 27:56, Mark 15:40, and John 19:25, it seems that Salome was the wife of Zebedee and the sister of Mary (the mother of Jesus). If this reasoning is accurate, then Salome was the mother of James and John and the aunt of Jesus. It is also possible that these verses name more than just four women at the Cross.

seems to favor this second possibility. In both accounts, Jesus asked James and John if they could "drink the cup" that He would drink. They claimed that they could. Then Jesus told them it was not His decision to make. This was followed by the other disciples getting upset with James and John. Finally, Jesus taught them about humility.

Conclusion

Since both of the examples above are plausible, there is no need to accuse the Bible of being in error here. These two Gospel accounts are complementary rather than contradictory.

Figuring out the Root of the Matter

← John Bartlett Jr. →

Did the fig tree wither immediately?

The "Problem"

The following passages give us some of the context for this supposed contradiction.

> And seeing a fig tree by the road, He [Jesus] came to it and found nothing on it but leaves, and said to it, "Let no fruit grow on you ever again!" Immediately the fig tree withered away (Matthew 21:19).

> Now in the morning, as they passed by, they saw the fig tree dried up from the roots. And Peter, remembering, said to Him, "Rabbi, look! The fig tree which You cursed has withered away" (Mark 11:20–21).

If these passages were speaking *fig*uratively, then we wouldn't be worried about the apparent contradiction between these two accounts of the Lord's encounter with a fig tree in Matthew 21:19 and Mark 11:20. Howbeit, we are dealing with a passage in a literal sense.

We know that Jesus literally caused the fig tree to wither. Thus, there seems to be a problem in the timing. At first reading, it appears that the tree withered at once in Matthew, but according to Mark it withered the day after Jesus rebuked it. How could the fig tree wither immediately and on the next day as well?

The Solution

At first, it might seem like Jesus could have told a fig tree to wither on two different occasions, right? Well, given the context, it is most likely that Matthew and Mark were writing about the same occasion — especially because both instances would have had to occur on the same day.

In Matthew 21:17 we read, "Then He left them [chief priests and the scribes] and went out of the city to Bethany, and He lodged there." The very next verses state, "Now in the morning, as He returned to the city, He was hungry. And seeing a fig tree by the road, He came to it and found nothing on it but leaves" (Matthew 21:18–19). Similarly, Mark recorded, "And Jesus went into Jerusalem and into the temple. So when He had looked around at all things, as the hour was already late, He went out to Bethany with the twelve. Now the next day, when they had come out from Bethany, He was hungry. And seeing from afar a fig tree having leaves, He went to see if perhaps He would find something on it" (Mark 11:11–13).

Both passages describe Jesus encountering the fig tree on the day after His triumphal entry into Jerusalem (see Matthew 21:1–11 and Mark 11:1–10). There are at least three plausible solutions to this dilemma, and now that we understand the timing of the event, let's dig deeper into the wording of both accounts. Take a look at this parallel passage to Matthew 21:19:

> And seeing from afar a fig tree having leaves, He went to see if perhaps He could find something on it. When He came to it, He found nothing but leaves, for it was not the season for figs. In response Jesus said to it, "Let no one eat fruit from you ever again." And His disciples heard it (Mark 11:13–14).

I can just imagine the disciples thinking, *That was strange. Jesus should know that figs come later in the season.* Of course, Jesus knew that — He created the fig tree.

Jesus used this opportunity to make an important point. Many scholars believe the fig tree represented Israel, or at least her leaders in Jerusalem, since fruitless fig trees are often used symbolically in reference to judgment (Jeremiah 8:13; Joel 1:7). If this is accurate, then Jesus was showing what would soon come to pass as God's judgment would fall on the nation. Others understand this event as symbolizing that, much like the fig tree's lack of fruit, you can also recognize followers of Christ by their good fruit, discern hypocrites by their lack of fruit, and false teachers by their bad fruit.

Mark went on to write the following words:

> Now in the morning, as they passed by, they saw the fig tree dried up from the roots. And Peter, remembering, said to Him, "Rabbi, look! The fig tree which You cursed has withered away."
>
> So Jesus answered and said to them, "Have faith in God. For assuredly, I say to you, whoever says to this mountain, 'Be removed and be cast into the sea,' and does not doubt in his heart, but believes that those things he says will be done, he will have whatever he says. Therefore I say to you, whatever things you ask when you pray, believe that you receive them, and you will have them (Mark 11:20–24).

The passage recounts how Peter remembered and said to Jesus that the fig tree had withered to its roots. Matthew accounts for when the tree actually withered (being withered in appearance from a loss of moisture), and the passage in Mark's Gospel states that Peter took note that the tree had withered all the way to the roots (meaning that the tree had at this point completely shriveled). So, from this perspective, both passages are in agreement.

The other possible solutions are largely based on the variant meanings of two key terms. The first of these possibilities focuses on the word "withered" and is closely related to the previous solution. When Matthew stated that the fig tree withered away, did he mean that it was completely shriveled within minutes or that the process of withering began right away? Matthew 21:20 states, "And when the disciples saw it, they marveled, saying, 'How did the fig tree wither away so soon?' " Looking at Mark's account, we learn that the disciples did not see the withered tree until the next morning.

So at first glance, there appears to be a discrepancy, but if this view is right, then Matthew simply wrote about this particular event from a topical approach rather than chronological, while Mark did the opposite.

Another possible solution is based on the notion that "immediately" in Matthew 21:19 is a relative timing word. Although it is primarily used to refer to something that happens within the next few moments after a prior event, it can be used in a more relative sense in certain contexts that would normally require a long period of time. In this case, the withering of a tree would normally become noticeable over the period of weeks or several months. So if the fig tree withered overnight, Matthew's use of the word "immediate" would make sense.

Conclusion

If you ever doubt the text of Scripture, be sure to take the time to dig deeper. By taking one look at these passages, it would be easy to get confused and be discouraged. A more detailed study serves to demonstrate the trustworthiness of God's Word. Remember, many people are always eager to throw out the Word of God. Don't be so quick to follow their example. We know that so many passages have proved accurate, so we should give Scripture the benefit of the doubt when we come across a difficult passage.

Was Jesus Wrong About Zechariah's Father?

← Tim Chaffey →

Two people; two events?

Jesus said that Zechariah's father was named Berechiah, but 2 Chronicles states that Jehoiada was the father of Zechariah. Was Jesus mistaken?

The "Problem"

In Matthew 23, Jesus condemned the scribes and Pharisees for their hypocrisy. He concluded His rebuke with some especially strong statements.

> "Therefore you are witnesses against yourselves that you are sons of those who murdered the prophets. Fill up, then, the measure of your fathers' guilt. Serpents, brood of vipers! How can you escape the condemnation of hell? Therefore, indeed, I send you prophets, wise men, and scribes: some of them you will kill and crucify, and some of them you will scourge in your synagogues and persecute from city to city, that on you may come all the righteous blood shed on the earth, from the blood of righteous Abel to the blood of Zechariah, son of Berechiah, whom you murdered between the temple and the altar" (Matthew 23:31–35).

Jesus clearly stated that Zechariah, the son of Berechiah, was murdered between the temple and the altar. Second Chronicles reveals that Zechariah, the son of Jehoiada, was stoned "in the court of the house of the LORD" (2 Chronicles 24:21). So was Zechariah the son of Berechiah or the son of Jehoiada? How can we answer this supposed Bible contradiction?

Popular Answer

Many Christians have attempted to address this alleged contradiction by claiming that the Hebrew word for "son" (*ben*) can refer to both immediate and distant descendants. In other words, perhaps Jesus referred to the father of Zechariah, whereas the writer of 2 Chronicles referred to Zechariah's grandfather. While it is true that the Hebrew language permits such a usage for this word, this is not an adequate solution in this case, as I will argue below.

The Solution

Study Bibles often provide verses for the purpose of cross-referencing passages. In this case, several Bibles link Matthew 23:35 and 2 Chronicles 24:20. However, while there are several similarities in these accounts, the Bible provides the details to show us that these are two separate accounts. Remember, similarity does not necessarily equal "same-ness."

In this particular case, we know the name of the grandfather of Zechariah (the son of Berechiah). Jesus referred to the prophet whose prophecies have been preserved for us in the Book of Zechariah. The first verse of that book states, "In the eighth month of the second year of Darius, the word of the LORD came to Zechariah the son of Berechiah, the son of Iddo the prophet" (Zechariah 1:1). So the man to whom Jesus referred was the grandson of a man named Iddo (not Jehoiada), and his ministry as prophet began in the second year of Darius. This places the start of Zechariah's ministry around 520 B.C.[1]

The events in 2 Chronicles 24 took place during the latter years of the reign of Joash, king of Judah (ca. 835–796 B.C.). This means that Zechariah the son of Jehoiada lived roughly three centuries earlier than the son of Berechiah.

---

1. Dates for Zechariah and Joash from John C. Whitcomb, *Chart of Old Testament Kings and Prophets*. Available on certain versions of Logos Bible Software. James Ussher in *The Annals of the World* places Joash's reign from 878 B.C. and his death at 825 B.C., but agrees that the later Zechariah began his ministry at 520 B.C. Either date for Joash shows these are clearly two different people separated by hundreds of years.

So the solution to this supposed contradiction is that Jesus did not refer to the events of 2 Chronicles 24. Instead, He was speaking about the murder of the prophet Zechariah, the son of Berechiah, the son of Iddo. This makes sense in light of the context. Jesus told the scribes and Pharisees that they were guilty of all the righteous blood that had been shed on earth by their forefathers, "from the blood of righteous Abel to the blood of Zechariah" (Matthew 23:35). Abel was the first person to be murdered, and both Jesus and the writer of Hebrews identify him as righteous (Hebrews 11:4). Zechariah the son of Berechiah lived near the end of the Old Testament.

By citing the first and last martyrs of the Old Testament, Jesus essentially assigned guilt of the murder of every prophet to the scribes and Pharisees. If He had referred to Zechariah the son of Jehoiada, then Jesus would have missed out on another 300 years of history in which several prophets were martyred.

Once again, we see that there is no contradiction. We just needed to dig a little bit deeper to find the solution.

A Modern Example

This solution might raise the following objection from the critic: Do you expect me to believe that two people with the same name were both killed in a similar fashion? Actually, it is not uncommon for two people who share a name to experience similar events in life.

Consider, for example, that President George Bush of the United States of America led his nation into war in Iraq in 1991. Wait a minute! That can't be true, because President George Bush of the United States of America led his nation into war in Iraq in 2003. Actually, both are true. President George H.W. Bush led the United States in the Gulf War in 1991. His son, President George W. Bush, led the United States in the Iraq War in 2003. These two men share both first and last names and both led their same nation into war with Iraq during their presidencies.

So maybe it isn't too difficult after all to believe that two people with the same name can experience similar events.

Conclusion

This supposed contradiction can easily be answered when one studies the contexts of the relevant passages. This case also brings up an important point. The footnotes, text notes, and cross-reference notes provided in study Bibles are not inspired. Though these marginal notes are often very helpful, we must never forget that they are merely study aids developed by men, and they are far from inerrant and infallible. In this case, certain Bibles have, through cross-reference notes, misled readers to think that these two accounts referred to the same person and events.

Jesus was not mistaken when He claimed that Zechariah was the son of Berechiah. Nor was the writer of 2 Chronicles mistaken when he stated that Zechariah was the son of Jehoiada. Both were accurate because both Zechariahs were murdered in or near the temple. And both Bible passages are accurate, because they are inspired by the God of truth, who never contradicts Himself. That's why we can always trust Him and not cave in to skeptics.

When Was the Temple Veil Torn in Two?

⤝ Tim Chaffey ⤞

Before . . . at the same moment . . . after?

Matthew and Mark state that the temple veil ripped right after Jesus died, but Luke states that it happened before the Lord's death.

The "Problem"

The Gospel accounts seem to disagree as to when the temple veil was torn in two in relation to Christ's death. A quick look at the relevant passages will highlight this supposed contradiction.

> And Jesus cried out again with a loud voice, and yielded up His spirit.
> Then, behold, the veil of the temple was torn in two from top to bottom; and the earth quaked, and the rocks were split (Matthew 27:50–51).

> And Jesus cried out with a loud voice, and breathed His last.
> Then the veil of the temple was torn in two from top to bottom (Mark 15:37–38).

> Then the sun was darkened, and the veil of the temple was torn in two. And when Jesus had cried out with a loud voice, He said, "Father, 'into Your hands I commit My spirit.' " Having said this, He breathed His last (Luke 23:45–46).

The Solution

At first glance, the differences between these passages may seem irreconcilable. However, there is a plausible solution which demonstrates that these passages are complementary rather than contradictory.

Before presenting this explanation, we can use these verses to dispel a common myth. Some people have claimed that the authors of the Gospel accounts (especially Matthew, Mark, and Luke) are guilty of collusion. That is, these men got together prior to writing their records and made sure that they had all of the details ironed out. However, when we come across these alleged discrepancies, it reveals to us that the writers were not in collusion because they would have likely used the same words in the same order to prevent any of these supposed contradictions from appearing.

There is a rather simple resolution to this issue: the temple veil tore at the same moment Jesus died. If three eyewitnesses were to record two simultaneous events, would they be forced to list the occurrences in the same order? Of course not. The individuals would be allowed to choose which one to report first. In this case, Matthew and Mark chose to highlight the death of Christ before mentioning the tearing of the temple veil. Luke chose to mention the veil before reporting the death of Christ.

But doesn't Luke clearly state that Jesus died after the temple veil was torn? No, he doesn't, but it appears that way in some English translations. This is one of the difficulties of the translation process. In each of the passages, the word translated as "then" is the Greek word "καὶ" (*kai*). This particle is a conjunction which can have either a copulative or cumulative force.[1] In other words, this word can be used to join together two words or groups of words, and it can also be used when the writer wants to build one idea upon another. The word is often translated as "and," "also," "even," "both," "then," "so," or "likewise."

The versions that translate *kai* as "then" seem to give the impression that one of these events happened and then the other event occurred; hence, the apparent contradiction.[2] However, many

---

1. James Strong, *The Exhaustive Concordance of the Bible*, electronic ed. (Ontario: Woodside Bible Fellowship, 1996), s.v., καὶ.

2. Even those that translate the word as "then" do not necessarily force a contradiction into the text. It is possible to interpret verses 44–45 as a summary statement of the setting while verse 46 focuses on Christ's final words which took place at the end of the three hours mentioned in the previous verses.

Bibles translate *kai* as "and."[3] This rendering reinforces the idea that Christ's death and the tearing of the temple veil took place at the same time.

It's a Big Deal

Some readers may wonder if this issue is important. Of course, if this was an actual contradiction, then we could not claim the Bible to be the inerrant Word of God. But there is another point that must be mentioned.

The Book of Hebrews goes into great detail about the superiority of Christ and His ministry as High Priest when compared to the Levitical system and its priests. "This hope we have as an anchor of the soul, both sure and steadfast, and which enters the Presence behind the veil, where the forerunner has entered for us, even Jesus, having become High Priest forever according to the order of Melchizedek" (Hebrews 6:19–20). The writer of Hebrews explained that Jesus has gone "behind the veil" for us, to serve as our High Priest. The tearing of the temple veil signified the start of Christ's ministry as High Priest. We no longer need to go through a regular priest to have access to God. We can go directly to Christ who now serves in that role.

In the Levitical system, the high priest offered daily sacrifices for the sins of the people (Hebrews 7:27), and once a year would go behind the veil to offer a sacrifice in the "Holy of Holies" (Hebrews 9:3, 7, NASB). The writer of Hebrews goes on to express the supremacy of Christ as our High Priest:

> But Christ came as High Priest of the good things to come, with the greater and more perfect tabernacle not made with hands, that is, not of this creation. Not with the blood of goats and calves, but with His own blood He entered the Most Holy Place once for all, having obtained eternal redemption (Hebrews 9:11–12).

---

3. For example, of the over 9,000 occurrences of this term in the Bible, the King James Version uses "and" 88 percent of the time, including each occurrence of the word in these passages.

Notice that Jesus entered the "Most Holy Place" (behind the veil) when He offered His own blood. In other words, Christ's ministry as High Priest began at His death. As such, the temple veil would have ripped at the moment of His death, not before it.

Conclusion

It does not make sense that the veil would have torn before the Lord's death on the Cross as some versions of Luke 23:45–46 seem to imply. However, if *kai* is translated as "and" (which is by far the most common rendering), then these events occurred simultaneously. Not only is this the best understanding of Matthew, Mark, and Luke, but it makes perfect sense with the theological point made in Hebrews that the temple veil tore at the very same moment that Jesus died.

First Impressions

✦ Tommy Mitchell ✦

Did Jesus first appear to the 11 disciples on a mountain in Galilee or in Jerusalem behind closed doors?

The "Problem"

The Gospels seem to provide conflicting information concerning the location of the Lord's first appearance to the 11 disciples following His Resurrection.

> Then the eleven disciples went away into Galilee, to the mountain which Jesus had appointed for them. When they saw Him, they worshiped Him; but some doubted (Matthew 28:16–17).

> Later He appeared to the eleven as they sat at the table; and He rebuked their unbelief and hardness of heart, because they did not believe those who had seen Him after He had risen (Mark 16:14).

> Then, the same day at evening, being the first day of the week, when the doors were shut where the disciples were assembled, for fear of the Jews, Jesus came and stood in the midst, and said to them, "Peace be with you." When He had said this, He showed them His hands and His side. Then the disciples were glad when they saw the Lord (John 20:19–20).

> So they rose up that very hour and returned to Jerusalem, and found the eleven and those who were with them gathered together, saying, "The Lord is risen indeed, and has appeared to Simon!" And they told about the things that had happened on the road, and how He was known to them in the breaking of bread.
> Now as they said these things, Jesus Himself stood in the midst of them, and said to them, "Peace to you." But they were terrified and frightened, and supposed they had seen a spirit (Luke 24:33–37).

Does Matthew's account contradict those of the other gospel writers?

The Solution

Jesus made numerous appearances after His Resurrection. A quick survey of these appearances will show why these accounts are not contradictory but are actually complementary.

Each of the gospels includes an account of the women discovering the empty tomb. Jesus appeared to the group of women (Matthew 28:9–10) and to Mary Magdalene (John 20:16–17). He also appeared to two followers on the road to Emmaus, and then he appeared to Simon Peter alone, as recorded in Luke 24.

Jesus then made two appearances to the disciples gathered as a group behind closed doors in Jerusalem. The first of these appearances occurred on the evening of Resurrection Sunday and is mentioned by Luke and John. John reveals that Thomas missed out on the first appearance. Jesus returned eight days later to all 11 as recorded in the rest of John 20. Mark 16:14 records this later meeting with the 11. Jesus repeatedly upbraided His followers for not accepting the word of eyewitness accounts of His appearances. After all, He had already told them on several occasions that He would rise from the dead.

When the angels in the empty tomb and Jesus Himself gave the women messages for His followers, they included a promise that He would see them in Galilee at the place He had appointed. He had prophesied of His coming death and Resurrection, and He had even told His followers where in Galilee they would see Him again. In Matthew 28, both the angels and Jesus gave the women this message to deliver. Then, after a few verses describing how the Jewish leaders tried to cover up the Resurrection, Matthew 28:16 states that the 11 went to Galilee.

Scripture records two post-Resurrection appearances in Galilee. One is the meeting with seven disciples on the shores of the Sea of Tiberias (Sea of Galilee). The other is the appearance recorded in Matthew 28:16–17. There is no indication of how much time had elapsed between the initial appearances in the Jerusalem area, but at a minimum, there had to have been eight days plus travel time. If the meeting on the lakeshore had also occurred before the appearance on the mountain, then even more time would have passed. The Galilean appearance is logically placed as it follows the two promises about the event mentioned both by angels and the Lord.

Who was present at this meeting on the mountain in Galilee? The 11 were certainly there, but nothing in these verses suggests that they were the only ones. This appearance was very likely the event recorded in 1 Corinthians 15:6 when Christ appeared to more than five hundred brethren at once. Given that a significant amount of time had passed since the Resurrection, hundreds of followers could have received word of the promised appearance and arrived at the pre-arranged place on a mountain there in Galilee.

The verses tell us that the people worshiped Him, but some were doubtful. By this time, Jesus had appeared to the Apostles as a group at least twice in Jerusalem, and He appeared to 7 of them on the lakeshore. Despite their poor earlier performance, it is unlikely that any of the 11 were still in doubt, but it would not be at all surprising to initially find some lingering doubts in the five hundred. Jesus then told this large group to go and tell the world about Him, just as He had commissioned the smaller gathering of followers back in Jerusalem.

The mountain meeting in Galilee recorded in Matthew 28 was not the final appearance of Jesus. He still had to meet with His half-brother James, according to the passage in 1 Corinthians, as well as all of the Apostles. Finally, after 40 days of intermittent appearances (quite possibly more than those recorded, Acts 10:40), Jesus led His Apostles as far as Bethany on the eastern slope of Mount Olivet, not far from Jerusalem, and He ascended into heaven.

Conclusion

Thus, we can easily see that Matthew 28:16–17 does not contradict the other passages. The accounts in Mark, Luke, and John deal with events in Jerusalem on Resurrection Sunday and then eight days later. The appearance in Matthew 28 happens later when the 11 and probably hundreds of other followers had traveled to a pre-arranged mountain in Galilee to see their Lord reappearing as He had promised.

Wilderness or Wedding?

← Ron Dudek →

Was Jesus in the wilderness or at the wedding in Cana three days after His baptism?

The "Problem"

Mark's Gospel claims Jesus was "immediately" driven into the wilderness after His baptism, but John seems to disagree.

> Immediately the Spirit drove Him into the wilderness. And He was there in the wilderness forty days, tempted by Satan, and was with the wild beasts; and the angels ministered to Him (Mark 1:12–13).

However, in his Gospel, John seems to say that Jesus was in Cana three days after His baptism.

Is there a contradiction?

The Solution

Anyone seriously and honestly seeking to discover the truth should always begin by carefully examining the texts to discover exactly what they have to say to us. We should never read our own ideas into the text, but we should rather read them with the intention of finding the author's intended meaning. This is called exegesis. With this in mind, let's take a closer look at what the Gospel of Mark states concerning the timing surrounding Jesus' baptism.

> It came to pass in those days that Jesus came from Nazareth of Galilee, and was baptized by John in the Jordan. And immediately, coming up from the water, He saw the heavens parting and the Spirit descending upon Him like a dove. Then a voice came from heaven, "You are My beloved Son, in whom I am well pleased." Immediately the Spirit drove Him into the wilderness. And He was

there in the wilderness forty days, tempted by Satan, and was with the wild beasts; and the angels ministered to Him (Mark 1:9–13).

Five events stand out in the above account.

1. Jesus was baptized by John.

2. The Spirit descended on Jesus like a dove.

3. The Father spoke from heaven.

4. Jesus was driven into the wilderness.

5. Jesus was tempted by Satan in the wilderness for 40 days.

These five points seem to flow as a play-by-play chronology, with little or no room for long gaps between them. Therefore, it can be derived from a plain reading of the text that Jesus was indeed in the wilderness within a very short time after his baptism. This order of events is also portrayed in Matthew and Luke. As such, it is highly unlikely that He could have been in Cana three days after His baptism.

To solve this alleged problem it is necessary to read the entire record of John's account.

> Now this is the testimony of John, when the Jews sent priests and Levites from Jerusalem to ask him, "Who are you?"
>
> He confessed, and did not deny, but confessed, "I am not the Christ."
>
> And they asked him, "What then? Are you Elijah?"
>
> He said, "I am not."
>
> "Are you the Prophet?"
>
> And he answered, "No."
>
> Then they said to him, "Who are you, that we may give an answer to those who sent us? What do you say about yourself?"
>
> He said: "I am 'The voice of one crying in the wilderness: "Make straight the way of the Lord," ' as the prophet Isaiah said."
>
> Now those who were sent were from the Pharisees (John 1:19–24).

This entire account was written in the past tense. It is therefore describing events that had already taken place from the perspective of John the Apostle. Verses 32–33 mention the baptism of Jesus.

And John bore witness, saying, "I saw the Spirit descending from heaven like a dove, and He remained upon Him. I did not know Him, but He who sent me to baptize with water said to me, 'Upon whom you see the Spirit descending, and remaining on Him, this is He who baptizes with the Holy Spirit' " (John 1:32–33).

Again, the Apostle John recorded this as a past tense account of what John the Baptist had already done. John the Baptist was then describing these events to the people listening to his teaching and being baptized.

The alleged problem arises in the second chapter.

On the third day there was a wedding in Cana of Galilee, and the mother of Jesus was there. (John 2:1)

Skeptics mistakenly claim that John was referring to the third day after Christ's baptism. However, this part of John's Gospel, though chronological, is not an event-by-event account as is Mark 1:9–13. John's Gospel allows for gaps (i.e., other events to have taken place) in between the events recorded.

To summarize the events, Jesus was baptized by John the Baptist as described in Mark 1:9–11. He then immediately spent 40 days in the wilderness where He was tempted by Satan. After that, He returned to the area where John was baptizing. John 1:29 states that Jesus returned and the day after John the Baptist was questioned by the Jews. John the Baptist identified Him again as the Messiah using very similar language, as we would expect for a prophet referring back to ideas written by previous prophets.

The next day John the Baptist again identified Jesus as "the Lamb of God" (John 1:35–36). Jesus then proceeded to interact with Andrew, Simon, Philip, and Nathanael while on His way to Galilee (John 1:37–51). Three days after those events, Jesus was at the wedding in Cana of Galilee where He performed the first public miracle of His earthly ministry (John 2:1–11).

Conclusion

Therefore, without doing any harm to the text, we can conclude the wedding at Cana took place after Jesus had returned from His 40 days in the wilderness and three days after He called the disciples as described in John 1:35–51. There is no contradiction when we carefully examine the various accounts in the Gospels.

Cock-a-doodle,
One or Two?

← Bodie Hodge →

Did the cock crow once or twice?

The Problem

At Peter's denials of Christ, did the rooster crow once (Matthew 26:34; Luke 22:34; John 13:38) or twice (Mark 14:3) and how does this affect inspiration of Scripture?

To dive into the subject, let me first take you to Mark 13:35, which is relevant to the discussion. But let me explain it first. Perhaps this is due to my experiences on the chicken farm on which I grew up. The passage says:

> Watch therefore, for you do not know when the master of the house is coming — in the evening, at midnight, at the crowing of the rooster, or in the morning.

Jesus spoke these words in the context of teaching His followers to make sure they stayed alert so they could be found "watching when the master of the house is coming." He divided the night hours into four sections or "watches." According to Jewish practices during the time of Christ, "evening" lasted from about 6:00 p.m. to 9:00 p.m.; "midnight" was around 9:00 p.m. until 12:00 a.m.; "the crowing of the rooster" continued from about 12:00 a.m. until 3:00 a.m.; and "the morning" watch was approximately from 3:00 a.m. to 6:00 a.m.

We commonly use similar language in English but we usually leave out the "crowing of the rooster," as few people (in the United States anyway) live on farms and raise chickens, so we commonly say just use evening, midnight, and morning (sometimes we insert "early morning" to replace "the crowing of the rooster," if events occurred in those hours. Furthermore, from my experience on the farm, the "crowing of the rooster" time frame is not restricted to a particular hour. Instead, it lasts for several hours as the rooster crows off and on, and it can last from midnight until the morning hours, but is marked by the first rooster crow in the night.

I can sleep through this rather well, being accustomed to it. (My wife, on the other hand, despises roosters' crows, as I found out the first time we spent the night on the family farm together. She failed to sleep for the rest of the night, once the roosters began to crowing.) So roosters crow for a *big portion* of the night, not just once or twice; sometimes they crow once and other times they do it twice or three times in a row — one right after the other.

Typically, roosters crow, not because the sun is coming up, as some have been led to believe, but because of changes in temperature, noise, wind, etc. (As a side note, notice the prophecy about a cock crowing which signifies change, and relate this to Peter's change by his denials of Christ.)

The Solution

This was a long introduction to get to the "meat" of the issue, but it will come into play. Let's now analyze the verses in question:

Matthew

Jesus said to him, "Assuredly, I say to you that this night, before the rooster crows, you will deny Me three times" (Matthew 26:34).

Then he began to curse and swear, saying, "I do not know the Man!" Immediately a rooster crowed. And Peter remembered the word of Jesus who had said to him, "Before the rooster crows, you will deny Me three times." So he went out and wept bitterly (Matthew 26:74–75).

Mark

Jesus said to him, "Assuredly, I say to you that today, even this night, before the rooster crows twice, you will deny Me three times" (Mark 14:30).

But he denied it, saying, "I neither know nor understand what you are saying." And he went out on the porch, and a rooster crowed (Mark 14:68).

A second time the rooster crowed. Then Peter called to mind the word that Jesus had said to him, "Before the rooster crows twice, you will deny Me three times." And when he thought about it, he wept (Mark 14:72).

Luke

Then He said, "I tell you, Peter, the rooster shall not crow this day before you will deny three times that you know Me" (Luke 22:34).

But Peter said, "Man, I do not know what you are saying!" Immediately, while he was still speaking, the rooster crowed. And the Lord turned and looked at Peter. And Peter remembered the word of the Lord, how He had said to him, "Before the rooster crows, you will deny Me three times" (Luke 22:60–61).

John

Jesus answered him, "Will you lay down your life for My sake? Most assuredly, I say to you, the rooster shall not crow till you have denied Me three times (John 13:38).

Peter then denied again; and immediately a rooster crowed (John 18:27).

All four Gospels record a prophecy about a cock (rooster) crowing at or around the time of Peter's third denial. Each also record that this sound triggered Peter to remember the prophecy. Matthew, Luke, and John were not being specific about how many times the cock crowed nor did they make the case that it was the first time or the *only* time the cock crowed. It seems they were making the point of *significance*, that is, when Peter heard a particular cock crowing, this prophecy would come to mind.

Mark adds a detail not found in the other accounts — that Peter would deny Christ before the cock crowed twice. We should expect Mark to include extra details about Peter, because he was basically a scribe for Peter as early church fathers attest. He recorded what he learned *from Peter*. So if any of the Gospel writers were to fill in an extra detail about Peter on this event, Mark would be the one.

There are several plausible ways to show that it is not a contradiction with the other three gospel writers. Keep in mind that a contradiction is "A and not A in the same relationship at the same time." So a legitimate contradiction would be if the Gospel writers claimed the rooster crowed and did not crow at the same time in this situation, or if they claimed that *only* one rooster would crow and that *more than* one would crow — but that is clearly not what the Bible says. All four Gospels attest to a cock crowing at the time of Peter's third denial, and the other three do not say it was the only crow. So our goal is to show these accounts are complementary.

The first step in dealing with these supposed contradictions is to check the context of the passages. In this case, we find something very interesting. Matthew and Mark place Jesus and His disciples on the Mount of Olives during the giving of this prophecy. These two writers also have Jesus stating that all of the disciples would be made to stumble that night before Peter spoke up and pledged his allegiance to Jesus. At this point, Jesus told Peter that he would deny Him three times before the rooster crowed. On the other hand, Luke and John tell us that Jesus was already talking to Peter alone in the Upper Room *before* they left for the Mount of Olives.

So is this another point of disagreement among the Gospel writers? Not at all! The best solution to this dilemma is that Jesus told Peter about his coming denials while they were still in the Upper Room. Then when they went out to the Mount of Olives, Jesus told all of the disciples that they would stumble that night. At this point, Peter reiterated His promise to stand by Jesus no matter what the consequences. Jesus once again told Peter that he would deny the Savior three times "before the rooster crows" (Matthew 26:34).

With that point of clarification, we are still left with the supposed differences between Matthew and Mark. Did Jesus say the cock would crow once or twice? Some commentators, such as Dr. John Gill, have appealed to a copyist mistake. Beza's ancient copy that was given to Cambridge University does not have "twice" in Mark 14:30 nor does the Ethiopic version. If these accurately represent the original texts on this verse then the difficulty disappears.[1] A copyist mistake would not affect the doctrine of inerrancy, since that doctrine only applies to the original manuscripts.

Dr. Gill further argued that the meaning of the cock crowing referred to "the time of cock crowing."[2] Since the third watch of the night was known as the cock crowing, this time period would include one cock crowing or more than one crowing — but one would have to signify the beginning of this time frame. As such, this alleged contradiction dissolves when one understands more about the cultural setting in which Jesus spoke these words.

Another resolution to the alleged contradiction is realizing that the second crow mentioned by Mark was likely the same crow mentioned by Matthew, Luke, and John and was separated by enough time to be considered a single significant crow by these authors. The first two denials of Peter were done in response to a servant girl (Mark 14:66–67), and after the servant girl told others, a particular man confronted Peter the second time (Mark 14:69; Luke 22:59). The final denial was made approximately one hour later (Luke 22:59) in front of a crowd who stood near Peter (Mark 14:70; Matthew 26:73). This crowd included a relative of Malchus, the man whose ear Peter had sliced off earlier in the night (John 18:26). It is rather obvious by the context that Matthew, Luke, and John all reference the second rooster crow:

1. The crowing in Matthew is the same as the second crow in Mark. Notice that both mention Peter's cursing and swearing which occurred at the third denial and the second crowing in Mark 14:71–72; Matthew 26:74.

2. The crow that Luke mentions is the second crow in Mark because Luke 22:60 indicates the cock crowed after the

---

1. John Gill, *Commentary on the Bible*, notes Matthew 26:34, as adapted from Online Bible by Larry Pierce.

2. Ibid., notes John 13:38, as adapted from Online Bible by Larry Pierce.

third denial, which corresponds to the second crow in Mark.

3. The crow that John discusses is also the second crow in Mark. It occurred immediately following his third denial, but John also indicates that the first denial was separated from the second and the third denials by the length of Jesus' trial before Annas. Luke reveals that about one hour had passed between the first and final denials.

The fulfillment of the Lord's prophecies about Peter's denials are recorded by all four Gospel authors. The context of the fulfillment in Matthew, Luke, and John is not in reference to the first crow, but clearly refers to the second rooster crow, which was the significant crowing of the cock that caused Peter to remember the Lord's prophecy. The two crows were separated by about an hour, so the second crow can rightly be described by the words "the rooster crowed." These accounts are not contradictory; rather, they are complementary.

When Did Jesus Cleanse the Temple?

← Tim Chaffey →

The Gospel of John states that Jesus cleansed the temple early in His ministry, but the other Gospels place the temple-cleansing near the end of His ministry. Who is right?

The "Problem"

The second chapter of John explains that during the Passover, Jesus went to the temple in Jerusalem, made a whip of cords, and drove out the money changers who were doing business there. He also poured out the money and turned over the tables (John 2:13–15). Jesus said to those who sold doves, "Take these things away! Do not make My Father's house a house of merchandise!" (John 2:16).

The Synoptic Gospels (Matthew, Mark, and Luke) also tell of Jesus entering the temple, driving out those who bought and sold, overturning their tables, and telling the crowd that they had turned the temple into a "den of thieves" (Matthew 21:12–13; Mark 11:15–17; Luke 19:45–46).

Some Christians believe these accounts describe the same event, but there is a problem. John describes the cleansing of the temple as occurring during the first Passover (of three) mentioned in his Gospel. Meanwhile, Matthew, Mark, and Luke all describe the temple-cleansing as taking place just days before Christ's Crucifixion. Is this a contradiction and, if so, who is right?

The Solution

Students of the Bible need to realize that similarity does not necessarily equal same-ness. In other words, just because two accounts are similar, it does not mean they refer to the same thing. In this case, the solution is actually quite simple. Jesus cleansed the temple on at least two occasions. The first time was near the beginning of His ministry, as described in John. The final time was just prior to His death, as described in the Synoptics.

The critic might protest and suggest this is simply an *ad hoc* answer (i.e., a solution concocted just to address the objection), but the biblical accounts support this. Furthermore, the biblical authors should be given the benefit of the doubt. So rather than automatically crying "Contradiction!" we should see if a solution can be found.

The most obvious difference has already been explained. These events took place at different points of Christ's ministry.

When you look closely at these accounts other differences can be found. In John, Jesus was immediately confronted by temple officials who asked, "What sign do You show to us, since You do these things?" John revealed that the Lord responded by pointing to His future Resurrection: "Destroy this temple, and in three days I will raise it up" (John 2:19; cf. 2:22). There is no mention of this confrontation or Christ's prophecy in Matthew, Mark, or Luke.

In contrast to this, the Synoptics record that following the second cleansing, Jesus began to teach those who were in the temple and heal the blind and lame that came to Him.

John wrote that Jesus made a whip of cords and then drove out the money changers. The Synoptics do not mention a whip at all.

The words that Jesus spoke while cleansing the temple are different. As cited above regarding the first temple-cleansing, the Lord stated, "Take these things away! Do not make My Father's house a house of merchandise!" (John 2:16). However, during the second cleansing Jesus said, "It is written, 'My house shall be called a house of prayer,' but you have made it a 'den of thieves' " (Matthew 21:13; cf. Mark 11:17; Luke 19:46). While the message was similar, the words Jesus used to convey His message were different.

Would Jesus Really Do This Twice?

Some may wonder at the plausibility of Jesus cleansing the temple on two occasions, but there is no reason to doubt that He would do this. Remember, Jesus often confronted the religious leaders and challenged their hypocrisy. In this case, the money changers were guilty of turning worship into a matter of convenience while stealing from the people by charging exorbitant prices for substandard sacrificial animals. Instead of following God's command to offer pure, spotless lambs from their own flocks at Passover (Exodus 12:5), many Jews were guilty of commercializing this process. They simply traveled to Jerusalem and purchased animals from the market at the temple. This is not what the Lord commanded.

Jesus challenged these ungodly practices and urged the people to obey God rather than convenience. In doing so, He also angered Caiaphas, the high priest, whose family was in charge of the money changing in the temple. Not only did the Lord's actions challenge the authority of Caiaphas, they also hurt his family's financial holdings since they had grown rich from the sale of sacrificial animals.[1]

Just as the Old Testament revealed that God was zealous for true worship from His people, Jesus demonstrated that obedience is better than sacrifice. Since Annas and Caiaphas refused to shape up following the first temple-cleansing in John 2, Jesus took another opportunity to remind the people of the importance of true worship.

---

1. The respected historian Alfred Edersheim explained that both Josephus and the Rabbinic writings claim that Annas, the father-in-law of Caiaphas, was in charge of the "Temple-market." The Rabbinic writings referred to this market as the "Bazaars of the sons of Annas" while Josephus claimed that Annas (the son of the high priest Annas) was very rich and guilty of "despoiling by open violence the common priests of their official revenues." Alfred Edersheim, *The Life and Times of Jesus the Messiah*, Two Volumes in One, 8th edition (New York: Longmans, Green, and Co., 1896), p. 371–372.

Conclusion

The solution to this supposed Bible contradiction is rather straightforward. Jesus cleansed the temple on at least two occasions: once at the beginning and again at the end of His earthly ministry. This should not surprise us since God repeatedly stressed in His Word that it is more important to obey Him than it is to perform empty rituals, especially when those rituals are done for convenience or personal gain.

Addendum — Approaching a Difficulty: Why Our First Reaction Is not Necessarily Correct

When the above article appeared on our website, it led to several responses disagreeing with my conclusion that Jesus actually cleansed the temple twice — once near the start of His ministry and once near the end. Here are comments from two individuals, each promoting the notion that John described the same event as the Synoptic Gospels (Matthew, Mark, and Luke):

> Response #1: This has got to be one of the stupidest answers ever! The reality is that the writers remembered things differently. It would be very suspicious if they were all the same, as if they got together and invented the story. The fact is nobody remembers the same event the same way. And we should not expect the Bible to do so. They were inspired by the Holy Spirit, but that does not override the individuality of the writers.

> Response #2: I think it's more of a stretch to say these are two separate instances rather than just two different accounts of the same event. These gospels are given in parallel and about the same events as accounts inspired by God. It's silly to think each record accounted by different individuals would record the exact same dialog and story in complete entirety. Perhaps the accounts together give a more complete picture? I don't see these as contradictory, but instead complementary. I think at times we Christians try too hard to prove things that don't need to be proven and at times Christians come off as too apologetic to be right. I

unapologetically assume both are accurate representations of the same event.

When dealing with alleged contradictions in Scripture, we must remember several important principles. First, since the words of Scripture are God-breathed (yet still allowing the writers' styles, vocabularies, etc., to show), there were no contradictions in the original manuscripts. Second, our task is to provide one or more plausible solutions to the difficulty. Third, we need to study the issue in detail so that our response does not create even more problems.

When considering this particular difficulty, my first approach was to see if John was talking about the same event as the other authors. That would appear to be the easiest solution. As these two responses pointed out, the Gospel accounts are not always in chronological order. Also, they are correct that we should not expect the biblical writers to use the exact same wording when describing the same event. On these points, we are in agreement.

However, some serious problems arise if we adopt the position that these writers were simply recording the same event. This is why I proposed that John wrote about a temple cleansing near the beginning of the Lord's ministry while Matthew, Mark, and Luke wrote about an event near the end of the Lord's earthly ministry.

First, while John may not have been primarily concerned with chronology, he did use chronological terminology in this context, which rules out the possibility that these were the same events. John 2:13 opens John's account of Jesus cleansing the temple. The prior events in this Gospel took place in Galilee (the calling of the disciples, the wedding at Cana), and then the scene shifts to Jerusalem in this passage. The next passage is about Nicodemus visiting Jesus at night. Although it is not specifically stated in the passage where this event took place, it was almost certainly in or near Jerusalem. Nicodemus was a member of the Sanhedrin who would definitely have been in Jerusalem during the Passover, as he was during the Lord's final Passover (John 19:39). Keep in mind that the chapter breaks were a later insertion, so unless stated otherwise by the writer, there is no reason to assume any significant change in time or location. The clincher on this subject comes from John 3:22–24.

> *After these things* Jesus and His disciples came into the land of Judea, and there He remained with them and baptized. Now John also was baptizing in Aenon near Salim, because there was much water there. And they came and were baptized. For *John had not yet been thrown into prison.* (emphasis added)

The word translated as "these things" is the Greek word *tauta*, which is a plural pronoun (i.e., "these" — contrast with John 2:12, where the singular form of this pronoun, *touto*, is accurately translated as "this"). After what things? This must refer to at least the two previous accounts, which would be the temple cleansing and the meeting with Nicodemus. So it is *after these things* that Jesus went out to the Judean countryside[2] and His disciples baptized "more disciples than John [the Baptist]" (John 3:24; 4:1). John the Baptist was still alive! This means that the temple cleansing described in John's Gospel took place before John the Baptist was executed. The temple cleansing described in the Synoptics clearly took place immediately after Christ's triumphal entry into Jerusalem, which occurred after John the Baptist's death.

A second major problem arises if we take the position that all four Gospel writers described the same event. After Jesus cleansed the temple and prophesied about His Resurrection, the Jews said, "It has taken forty-six years to build this temple, and will You raise it up in three days?" (John 2:20). It's important to recognize that these words are not recorded in the Synoptic Gospels. If they were, then there would be critical difficulties with the biblical time-line.

According to Josephus, the restoration or rebuilding of the second temple began in the eighteenth year of Herod's reign (20

---

2. The phrase translated as "came into the land of Judea" literally means "into the Judean land." The ESV, NIV, HCSB, and others translate it as "the Judean countryside," which is the meaning conveyed by the Greek words. This is because Jesus and His disciples were already in Jerusalem (John 2:23), which was in the territory of Judea. So they could not really come into the land of Judea if they were already there. The context makes it clear that Jesus and His disciples moved from Jerusalem to the countryside.

or 19 B.C.).[3] If we add 46 years to this date it brings us to A.D. 27 or 28, but this is too early for the triumphal entry of Jesus. He was born around 5 or 4 B.C. and was "about thirty years of age" when He began His ministry (Luke 3:23). Thirty years from his birth would be approximately A.D. 26 or 27, which fits nicely with the 46 years from the rebuilding of the temple. But we still need to add to this the years for his ministry.[4] The Crucifixion likely occurred sometime between A.D. 30 and 33. Jesus did not enter Jerusalem during the triumphal entry 46 years after the renovation of the temple started.

Although the temple cleansings were similar in nature and result, we should not automatically assume they were the same event. Remember, similarity does not necessarily equal "same-ness." John's Gospel includes several distinctive features not included in the Synoptic Gospels. As such, a careful look at the text reveals that the best solution to this dilemma is to recognize Jesus cleansed the temple on at least two occasions.

---

3. Josephus stated that "Herod, in the eighteenth year of his reign, and after the acts already mentioned, undertook a very great work, that is, to build of himself the temple of God, and make it larger." Josephus, *The Antiquities of the Jews*, 15.11.380. Jones places the eighteenth year of Herod's reign as beginning in 20 B.C. Floyd Nolen Jones, *The Chronology of the Old Testament*, (Green Forest, AR: Master Books, 2005), p. 219. Ussher places the eighteenth year of Herod's reign in 19 B.C. James Ussher, *The Annals of the World*, revised edition, (Green Forest, AR: Master Books, 2003), p. 765–766.

4. There are many other timing issues that go into this calculation. We know the Lord's ministry lasted at least three Passovers (John 2:13; 6:4; 13:1), which means it had to have been longer than two years. It could have been even longer if John omitted one or more of the Passover celebrations during Christ's ministry. Also, John the Baptist's ministry began in the fifteenth year of the reign of Tiberius Caesar, but this is a difficult date to fix. If we start it when he became joint ruler with his father Augustus, then the fifteenth year was around A.D. 26 or 27, which, once again fits perfectly with the above dates. If we start from the year Augustus died, then John's ministry wouldn't have started until about A.D. 29. The Lord's ministry obviously began after John's.

Acts –
Revelation

Can a Thief Go to Heaven?

← Dan Lietha →

The Bible states that thieves will not inherit the kingdom of God, but Jesus told a thief that he would be with Him in Paradise.

The "Problem"

> Do you not know that the unrighteous will not inherit the kingdom of God? Do not be deceived. Neither fornicators, nor idolaters, nor adulterers, nor homosexuals, nor sodomites, nor thieves, nor covetous, nor drunkards, nor revilers, nor extortioners will inherit the kingdom of God (1 Corinthians 6:9–10).

In the verses above, we see a list of unrighteous people — sinners. It is stated twice that such people will not inherit the kingdom of God.

Included in this list are thieves. So why did Jesus, as described in Luke 23:39–43, promise to one of the thieves that was crucified with Him, "Assuredly, I say to you, today you will be with Me in Paradise"?

The Solution

Sometimes the answer to a seeming contradiction is so close that it would "bite you" if it could. This is the case here. Look at the very next verse in 1 Corinthians 6 to find the resolution:

> And such *were* some of you. But you were *washed*, but you were *sanctified*, but you were *justified* in the name of the Lord Jesus and by the Spirit of our God (1 Corinthians 6:11, emphasis added).

First Corinthians 6 is written to Christians — followers of Jesus Christ who have had all of their many sins forgiven and *washed* away by the powerful cleansing blood of the crucified and risen Savior

(Revelation 1:5). Each believer is horribly flawed, and yet forgiven and living with the promise and hope of heaven (Titus 3:7).

"And such *were* some of you" indicates this list of sins is a record of their past, but they repented (Acts 3:19) and had been freed from the bondage of their sin (Romans 6:5–23). God no longer held these or any other sins against them because they had been *sanctified* and *justified* in the name of Jesus Christ and by the Holy Spirit (Romans 3:24–26). Regardless of what kinds of sins they had committed, their record of wrongs had been wiped clean.

In the account of the thieves who were crucified with Christ, the same thing took place. One thief rejected Christ and remained in his unrighteous and unworthy state. The other thief recognized Christ as Savior and turned to Him for salvation, thereby becoming washed, sanctified, and justified before God. He became acceptable in the sight of God, because of the finished work of Christ, to inherit the Kingdom of God.

Thieves are thought of as "bad" people. Many people would not place themselves in the same category. However, how many times does one have to steal something to become a thief? Only once.

And who among us has not taken something, even the smallest thing, that did not belong to us? We are all thieves. We are all unrighteous lawbreakers, unworthy to inherit the kingdom of God (Romans 3:23). So the question, "Can a thief go to heaven?" applies to all of us.

Conclusion

The thieves crucified with Jesus are a fitting picture of all mankind. They show us the only two possible options for entering eternity: to receive Christ's free gift of salvation or reject it. So there's good news! When a thief receives Christ as Lord, he is no longer a thief in the eyes of God; his sin is covered and he is able to enter heaven. Scripture makes that plain and without contradiction.

Marriage — Good or Bad?

◈ Frost Smith ◈

*God said it was not good for man to be alone, so why
did Paul say it is good to remain single?*

The "Problem"

> Now concerning the things of which you wrote to me: It is
> good for a man not to touch a woman (1 Corinthians 7:1).

> For I wish that all men were even as I myself. But each one
> has his own gift from God, one in this manner and another in
> that. But I say to the unmarried and to the widows: It is good for
> them if they remain even as I am (1 Corinthians 7:7–8).

> And the LORD God said, "It is not good that man should
> be alone; I will make him a helper comparable to him" (Genesis
> 2:18).

> He who finds a wife finds a good thing, and obtains favor
> from the LORD (Proverbs 18:22).

Occasionally, we will get questions about whether marriage is
a bad thing because of what Paul says in 1 Corinthians 7:1, 7–8.
Yet Paul allows for marriage. Looking at the greater context in the
intervening verses, we see a reason Paul accepted marriage:

> Nevertheless, because of sexual immorality, let each man
> have his own wife, and let each woman have her own husband.
> . . . Do not deprive one another except with consent for a time,
> that you may give yourselves to fasting and prayer; and come
> together again so that Satan does not tempt you because of your
> lack of self-control. But I say this as a concession, not as a com-
> mandment (1 Corinthians 7:2–6).

So how can marriage be somehow not preferable or a concession in light of the verses we see in Genesis 2:18 and Proverbs 18:22?

The Solution

There is more to consider here than just marriage itself. Why does Paul think his (single) lot is better? In 1 Corinthians 7:33–35, Paul explains that being unattached is better for a Christian so "that you may serve the Lord without distraction." Paul's entire life was absorbed by service to the Lord. It would have been difficult for Paul to have been an undistracted husband and father with his calling. And, while we're told to "be fruitful and multiply" in Genesis 1:28, it is also a high calling, albeit not for everyone, to serve the Lord continually, as Anna was able to once she was widowed (Luke 2:36–37).

Matthew 19:11–12 discusses those who are not able to marry or have children for one reason or another. Sadly, many would consider this to be a disadvantage, but the Bible paints a different picture, noting that "All cannot accept this saying, but only those *to whom it has been given*" (emphasis added). Since "all things work together for good to those who love God," they are called to a high (His) purpose (Romans 8:28). And it has been given to those individuals the strength and privilege to be thus used by God (1 Corinthians 10:13). Not that it is always an easy path: Paul's path was beset with illness, discomfort (to say the least), disaster, contention, imprisonment, and finally death. Yet the Lord always sustained him, and Paul, in fact, felt honored to be persecuted for the sake of Christ (Colossians 1:24). Now, that's God-given strength!

So, with God there are two good paths. You can be single and serve Him wholeheartedly while not having to worry about neglecting a family. This is preferable if you are gifted with this ability. Or you can get married and raise children in the Lord if He provides children to you. If He does not give you children then you are freer than those with children to serve. God sets both the path and then allows provision to the individual for that path. Who can say that

His plan, whether or not it includes a spouse or children, is not perfect?

But why would God have said that it was not good for man to be alone, then, in Genesis 2? In the hours prior to this, the Lord had brought animals to Adam to name, partly to demonstrate that He had a special plan for Adam: a special "helper," not merely brought forth from the earth as the insufficient animals were, but specially formed from part of him by the hand of God and in His image. God wanted Adam to be fruitful and to multiply, yes, but He also wanted him to see that He had a special plan for man unlike the mere procreation of animals: marriage. God would later use marriage to symbolize the joining of the Church to His Son, Jesus Christ — a beautiful relationship where Jesus would demonstrate divine love by laying down His life for His Bride. This analogy was given in regards to the roles of husbands and wives in Ephesians 5:22–33.

Conclusion

So is marriage a good thing? Absolutely. It was instituted by God in a perfect world, but it is not for everyone. Also, if you are part of the Bride of Christ, you can clearly say "Yes, and amen." If you're not, you can still greatly benefit from the beautiful God-given gift of marriage as it was originally intended (sadly God's original plan for marriage[1] has been abandoned throughout the ages, causing untold misery). Also realize that although mankind does not deserve the favor of God, there is the good news[2] that you, too, can be welcomed into His family — to share eternity with the Creator of the universe. Praise the Lord for this undeserved love He so freely gives all who ask.

---

1. http://www.answersingenesis.org/get-answers/topic/family-marriage.

2. http://www.answersingenesis.org/about/good-news.

Who Gets the Blame for Original Sin — Adam or Eve?

← Georgia Purdom →

Genesis 3 states that Eve ate the fruit first, but Romans 5 states that Adam caused sin to enter the world.

The "Problem"

The Genesis account of the Fall indicates that Eve ate the fruit first. This has led many people throughout history and even in our modern times to believe that she was the person responsible for original sin. You have likely heard the old canard, "We wouldn't be in this mess [meaning the general sinfulness of our fallen world] if it weren't for a woman." But is that an accurate statement? Is Eve to blame for original sin?

> So when the woman saw that the tree was good for food, that it was pleasant to the eyes, and a tree desirable to make one wise, she took of its fruit and ate. She also gave to her husband with her, and he ate (Genesis 3:6).

This verse makes it clear that Eve was the first to eat from the tree of knowledge of good and evil. God had told Adam not to eat from the tree, but Eve also had knowledge of this (Genesis 3:2–3). Adam ate but only after Eve. From this verse alone it might be easy to think that Eve is indeed to blame for original sin since she sinned first. Some have said that verses in the New Testament also support the idea that Eve is to blame because Eve was deceived and Adam was not.

For Adam was formed first, then Eve. And Adam was not deceived, but the woman being deceived, fell into transgression (1 Timothy 2:13–14).

But I fear, lest somehow, as the serpent deceived Eve by his craftiness, so your minds may be corrupted from the simplicity that is in Christ (2 Corinthians 11:3)

The Solution

However, Eve being deceived does not necessarily imply that she is to blame for original sin. If anything it might be tempting to think the opposite — that because Eve was deceived while Adam knew full well what he was doing that his sin is worse, and he should be blamed. However, the Bible never states that Adam's sin was worse than Eve's. Both were punished for their sin (Genesis 3:16–19).

It is necessary to look at other passages in both the Old and New Testaments to understand why Adam is to blame for original sin rather than Eve.

Adam was created first from the dust of the ground, and Eve was created from a rib taken from Adam's side (Genesis 2:7, 21–22). From these verses and others in Genesis 1–3 it is clear that the husband was created to be the leader in the marital relationship and that the wife was created to be the helper (Genesis 2:18). As the leader, it was Adam's responsibility to protect and provide for his family. This leadership role was clearly demonstrated when God talked with Adam and Eve following their sin. Even though Eve sinned before Adam, God questioned Adam first (Genesis 3:9). This was because of the leadership role God ordained for husbands in marriage. Adam, as the leader of the family, was held responsible, not only for his own sin of eating from the tree, but also because he did not provide adequate protection for his wife, allowing her to sin.

In the New Testament, Adam is clearly presented as both progenitor and representative of all mankind. The following passages state that Adam is the person through whom sin and resulting death entered the world:

For since by man came death, by Man also came the resurrection of the dead. For as in Adam all die, even so in Christ all shall be made alive.

And so it is written, "The first man Adam became a living being." The last Adam became a life-giving spirit (1 Corinthians 15:21–22, 45).

Therefore, just as through one man sin entered the world, and death through sin, and thus death spread to all men, because all sinned.

But the free gift is not like the offense. For if by the one man's offense many died, much more the grace of God and the gift by the grace of the one Man, Jesus Christ, abounded to many.

For if by the one man's offense death reigned through the one, much more those who receive abundance of grace and of the gift of righteousness will reign in life through the One, Jesus Christ. Therefore, as through one man's offense judgment came to all men, resulting in condemnation, even so through one Man's righteous act the free gift came to all men, resulting in justification of life. For as by one man's disobedience many were made sinners, so also by one Man's obedience many will be made righteous (Romans 5:12, 15, 17–19).

Just as sin and death came through one man, Adam, it is also through one man, Jesus Christ, that grace and righteousness are given as free gifts to sinners. The naming of Christ as the Last Adam and the multiple comparisons of Adam to Christ would be invalid and nonsensical if original sin came through Eve.

Interestingly, although Eve was the first to sin, the solution to sin came through "her Seed" (Genesis 3:15). The Seed, Jesus Christ, was born of a virgin named Mary. He paid the price for sin and will redeem those who receive the salvation He offers.

Conclusion

Scripture makes it clear that that sin and death entered this world through Adam, and thus he is to blame for original sin.

Root of All Evil?

⇠ Erik Lutz ⇢

A problem of not carefully examining the words?

The "Problem"

Is money good or bad?

Have you ever heard the phrase, "Money is the root of all evil"? This expression is derived from a passage of Scripture.

> For the love of money is a root of all kinds of evil (1 Timothy 6:10).

However, the Bible includes other statements that seem to contradict this one, such as the following:

> . . . but money answers everything (Ecclesiastes 10:19).

How can money be evil and yet be the answer to everything?

The Solution

Before considering this supposed contradiction, we must first note what this verse does not state. Paul did not write that money is *the* root of all evil, or even that the love of money is *the* root of all evil, which would imply that greed is ultimately responsible for all evil done on the earth. Instead, we read that love of money is "*a* root of all kinds of evil." In other words, people do all sorts of evil deeds because of a controlling desire for money.

Scripture never calls money inherently evil. In fact, wealth is often portrayed throughout God's Word as a blessing from the Lord. For example, Psalm 112:3 describes the man who fears the Lord: "Wealth and riches are in his house, and his righteousness endures forever." This is not a promise that God will make every Christian rich. However, physical rewards in this life often accompany righteous living because God always blesses His people — sometimes in material ways. James reminded believers that all blessings are from God: "Every good gift and every perfect gift is from above, and comes down from the Father of lights" (James 1:17).

Many of the biblical patriarchs were men of great physical wealth, such as Abraham, who "was very rich in livestock, in silver, and in gold" (Genesis 13:2), and Job, "the greatest of all the people of the East" (Job 1:3). Likewise, Solomon did not ask God for riches, yet the Lord blessed Him with incredible wealth. "So King Solomon surpassed all the kings of the earth in riches and wisdom" (1 Kings 10:23). Clearly, God does not despise money, as He often gives it to believers who desire Him instead of physical riches.

Moreover, there are also many statements in Scripture about the usefulness of money, such as the above example cited from Ecclesiastes. It is helpful to remember that the Book of Ecclesiastes, like Proverbs, is part of a genre called wisdom literature. These books contain many wise sayings and observations about the world. Rather than making specific promises, the authors often record general principles. For example, consider the well-known words in Proverbs 22:6, "Train up a child in the way he should go, and when he is old he will not depart from it." This is not an absolute guarantee from God that children raised in a godly home will never turn away from following the Lord. Instead, Solomon concisely articulated the importance of biblical parenting — people with a solid upbringing in the Word of God are typically much more grounded in their faith.

Much of Ecclesiastes is based on the writer's observations of this fallen world. In fact, he used the phrase "under the sun" 29 times to describe situations on this earth, and five times he announced that "all is vanity." Thus, the writer's observation that "money answers everything" fits perfectly within the context. Certainly, this does not mean that money is the *best* answer or the right solution to every problem. Similarly, Proverbs 10:15 claims, "The rich man's wealth is his strong city; the destruction of the poor is their poverty." These are is simply wise statements about the nature of money and its uses "under the sun."

Although wealth can be a blessing, God's Word also gives numerous warnings about the misuse of money. Paul strongly cautioned Timothy about the danger of loving money because "those who desire to be rich fall into temptation and a snare, and *into* many foolish and harmful lusts which drown men in destruction and perdition" (1 Timothy 6:9; cf. 1 Timothy 6:17).

This tension between the positive and negative aspects of money is similar to that of other issues in Scripture, such as eating (e.g., Proverbs 23:1–3). Food is not inherently evil, and it was given to us as a blessing, but it can be harmful if we love it more than God. Wealth is the same way. As Jesus said, no one can serve two masters, so "you cannot serve God and money" (Luke 16:13, ESV).

Money is extremely alluring to our flesh because it seems to answer everything. The promise of having more always hangs before us, and many in the world give their lives chasing after the "life of luxury." Jesus told a parable about a rich man who planned to tear down his barns only to build larger ones to store his crops and goods. Jesus spoke of this man's foolishness since he was not "rich toward God" (Luke 12:16–21). Solomon also knew well how fleeting earthly riches are: "Do not toil to acquire wealth; be discerning enough to desist. When your eyes light on it, it is gone, for suddenly it sprouts wings, flying like an eagle toward heaven" (Proverbs 23:4–5, ESV).

Conclusion

Physical possessions cannot bring true, lasting joy — they are miniscule in comparison to the treasures of spiritual blessings God offers to those who love Him. Therefore, Christians should rightly use the money God gives us, but not love it, since it is only temporary. Consider the following words of Jesus:

> Do not lay up for yourselves treasures on earth, where moth and rust destroy and where thieves break in and steal; but lay up for yourselves treasures in heaven, where neither moth nor rust destroys and where thieves do not break in and steal. For where your treasure is, there your heart will be also (Matthew 6:19–21).

The Bible Tells Me So

⤺ David Chakranarayan ⤻

Is all Scripture inspired by God, or is some of it the opinion of the writers of Scripture?

The "Problem"

Paul wrote in 2 Timothy 3:16 that all Scripture is inspired of God. But in 1 Corinthians 7, Paul seemed to indicate he was giving his own opinion on a subject. This apparent contradiction concerns the doctrine of the inspiration of Scripture. Let's read the passages in question:

> All Scripture is given by inspiration of God, and is profitable for doctrine, for reproof, for correction, for instruction in righteousness (2 Timothy 3:16).

> But to the rest I, not the Lord, say: If any brother has a wife who does not believe, and she is willing to live with him, let him not divorce her. . . . Now concerning virgins: I have no commandment from the Lord; yet I give judgment as one whom the Lord in His mercy has made trustworthy. . . . A wife is bound by law as long as her husband lives; but if her husband dies, she is at liberty to be married to whom she wishes, only in the Lord. But she is happier if she remains as she is, according to my judgment — and I think I also have the Spirit of God (1 Corinthians 7:12, 25, 39–40).

The Solution

When writing 2 Timothy, Paul was nearing the end of his life and passing on the mantle of ministry to his "son in the faith," Timothy. There may have been a potential danger of Timothy weakening spiritually as he faced pressures from within the Church and persecution from the unregenerate world. Paul's concern for Timothy is evident in 2 Timothy 1:6 where Paul asks Timothy to "stir up" the gift of God.

As the pressure of church ministry and outside persecution increased, compromise and fear may have risen within the Church. Paul wanted Timothy to deal with these issues by using the authority of Scripture— hence the reason "for reproof, for correction, for instruction in righteousness" (2 Timothy 3:16). He told Timothy that Scripture is given by inspiration of God, literally meaning that it is "God breathed" or the "breath of God."

The writers of Scripture were used of the Holy Spirit as they communicated God's message with their own literary styles. "All Scripture" includes both Old and New Testaments (see also 1 Thessalonians 2:13).

Peter also gave full credence for inspiration to both Old and New Testaments (2 Peter 3:15–16). Peter made the same claim as Paul in 2 Timothy.

> Knowing this first, that no prophecy of Scripture is of any private interpretation, for prophecy never came by the will of man, but holy men of God spoke as they were moved by the Holy Spirit (2 Peter 1:20–21).

In the context of 1 Corinthians 7, Paul was dealing with the principles of marriage. The church of Corinth was under rebuke from Paul because they failed to live up to the standards of God's holiness. Their lives showed no spiritual difference between them and the unbelieving world.

Union in marriage between believers and unbelievers was not an issue that Jesus dealt with head on in His teachings recorded in the Gospels. In Mark 10, Jesus spoke about marriage and divorce and concluded by tracing marriage back to where God ordained it — Genesis. However, Jesus did not deal directly with the topic of marriage as it relates to believers married to unbelievers. Commentating on 1 Corinthians 7:12, John Macarthur stated:

What were Christian to do who were already married to unbelievers, possibly even to immoral and idolatrous pagans? Were they free to divorce the one to whom they were unequally yoked and then free either to live singly or marry a believer? Those were honest questions. In light of Paul's teaching that their bodies were members of Christ and were temples of the Holy Spirit (6:15–20), the Corinthian Christians were justifiably concerned about whether or not to maintain marital union with an unbeliever. Some may have thought that such a union joined Christ to Satan, defiling the believer and the children and dishonoring the Lord. The desire for a Christian partner would be very strong. Jesus had not taught directly about that problem, and so Paul says, "to the rest say I, not the Lord." That is not a denial of inspiration or an indication that Paul is only giving his own human opinion. It is only to say that God has not given any previous revelation on the subject, but Paul was now setting it forth.[1]

Conclusion

Paul, inspired by the Holy Spirit, wrote many of the books of the New Testament. In 2 Timothy 3:16, Paul encouraged Timothy by exhorting him to teach with the authority of Scripture because it is the Word of God. In 1 Corinthians 7:12, Paul was still writing under the inspiration of the Holy Spirit but was merely indicating that the Lord had not previously given revelation on that particular matter. We can confidently trust Scripture as God's revelation to us.

---

1. John MacArthur, *The MacArthur New Testament Commentary: 1 Corinthians* (Chicago, IL: Moody Press, 1996), p. 166.

A Lot of Righteousness

← Troy Lacey →

How could Lot be called righteous in 2 Peter 2:7–8 when he did so many bad things as recorded in Genesis 19?

The "Problem"

In Genesis 13:12 we read that Lot, after departing from Abram (later called Abraham), dwelt in the cities of the plain near Sodom. By the time of Genesis 14:12, Lot had been living in Sodom for some time and was carried away captive but rescued by Abraham. The wicked reputation of the town of Sodom was obviously known to Lot (Genesis 13:13), yet he chose to stay there in spite of this knowledge.

In Genesis 18, Abraham pleaded with God to spare Sodom for the sake of the righteous who dwelt there. Perhaps he hoped that Lot and his family had been a godly influence on the inhabitants and that some had repented and turned to the true God. God agreed to Abraham's request and promised to spare the city if only ten righteous people could be found.

Genesis 19:1 records that Lot was sitting in the gate of Sodom when the angels came, and he invited them to his house. When a mob of men came later that evening to molest Lot's guests (Genesis 19:8), Lot offered his daughters to the crowd in an attempt to satiate them. Providentially, he was prevented from doing so. The angels pulled Lot back into the house and blinded the mob (Genesis 19:10–11).

Then the angels told Lot to gather his family members and leave Sodom, but his sons-in-law ignored his warnings. By daybreak, Lot was still lingering. The angels brought him out of the city with only his wife and his two daughters who were there. Lot's positive impact on Sodom had been negligible, and soon his wife was to die looking back (probably in longing) toward Sodom's destruction (Genesis 19:12–26).

Sometime soon after being in Zoar, Lot began to fear for his life. He took his daughters and moved to the mountains where they lived in a cave (Genesis 19:30). It is here that we read of the plot by his two daughters where they got him drunk so they could lie with him and become pregnant by him (Genesis 19:31–38).[1]

Other than a few passing references, such as Christ's brief mention of him in Luke 17:28–29, Lot fades from the pages of Scripture until 2 Peter 2:7–8. There we read that Lot was considered righteous and that he was vexed living among such wicked people as the people of Sodom and Gomorrah. How can we reconcile this in our minds? Lot, the ineffective leader, the indecisive family man, the comfort-loving hedonist, the drunken dad — how could this man be called righteous?

The Solution

Perhaps we judge Lot too harshly and forget the words of the Apostle Paul who after going through a long list of sins reminded the Corinthian church that "such were some of you. But you were washed, but you were sanctified, but you were justified in the name of the Lord Jesus and by the Spirit of our God" (1 Corinthians 6:11).

We only know of Lot's actions during a short period of his life. We are not told of Lot's final days, but we do know that while living with Abraham he was a witness to Abraham's humility, kindness, and faithfulness to God (Genesis 12:1–4; 13:8–9). He also saw Abraham make poor decisions and sin, and then saw him repent (Genesis 12:12–20; 13:1–5). So it is not unreasonable to presume that Lot repented of his sin later in life, and God forgave him as He has promised (1 John 1:9).

It is apparent from the text in 2 Peter that Lot was considered righteous. He was weak, and he sinned, but he did love the Lord.

---

1. Note that the laws forbidding sexual relationships between close relations were not codified until the time of Moses in Leviticus 18. Abraham married his half-sister, and Adam's and Eve's children married each other. Either way, these actions were carried out by the daughters, who were never called righteous by the Scriptures.

He did try to call out the people of Sodom for their sin by reminding them that they were doing wicked deeds (Genesis 19:7), and he tried to protect his angelic visitors. He may have been an ineffective evangelist, but he was burdened and grieved over the sin he saw around him.

Conclusion

What can the lesson of Lot's life teach us today? Although we live in a sinful world that hates God, we are not to be conformed to this world, but by God's grace we are to be transformed by the renewing of our mind (Romans 12:2). Lot, however, had a choice; he could have chosen to live outside the gates of the city, raised his family in a more godly way, and still attempted to have told the people of Sodom about the true and living God. The fact is that he did not do this, and his family was influenced by the wicked culture around them, even as Lot was tormented by it. The point can best be summed up by 1 Corinthians 15:33. "Do not be deceived: 'Evil company corrupts good habits.' "

Lot spent too much time around the creature comforts of life in Sodom, and consequently his testimony was tarnished. Yet even in all of this, God was faithful and did not forget that Lot was His servant. God twice delivered him physically, and through the Holy Spirit He conveyed to us that Lot was righteous, signifying more importantly that He delivered Lot from his sins (Galatians 1:4; 2 Timothy 4:18). Though Lot did not live a very outwardly righteous life, he believed in God by faith, and God counted that faith as righteousness.

To Die or Not to Die

✦ David Wright ✦

Did Enoch die as Hebrews 11:13 seems to imply or was he taken as stated in Genesis 5:24 and Hebrews 11:5?

The "Problem"

Skeptics will look in every nook and cranny of Scripture trying to find a "contradiction." And in order to do this, logic and simple grammatical comprehension must be thrown out the window. Now let's look at the passages in question.

> And Enoch walked with God; and he was not, for God took him (Genesis 5:24).

> By faith Enoch was taken away so that he did not see death, "and was not found, because God had taken him"; for before he was taken he had this testimony, that he pleased God (Hebrews 11:5).

So we see that Enoch did not die, or did he?

> These all died in faith, not having received the promises, but having seen them afar off were assured of them, embraced them and confessed that they were strangers and pilgrims on the earth (Hebrews 11:13).

The Solution

On the surface it would appear we have two contradicting statements only a few sentences apart. But there are a couple of ways of looking at this supposed conundrum.

First, there is a simple theological explanation. In Hebrews 11, there appears to be a division of main ideas presented in verses 1–5 and verses 6–13. Notice that verse 13 states, "These all died in faith, not having received the promises." What promises? When we look back on verses 7–11 we see that each person who is mentioned received and believed a promise, so verse 13 only refers to Noah, Abraham, Isaac, Jacob, and Sarah — *not* Enoch or Abel. Hebrews does not mention any promises concerning Enoch and Abel in verses 4–5. And the author specifically mentions Abel was dead and Enoch was not.

Second, there is a simple grammatical explanation. Enoch is the exception to the rule. The rule is that everyone listed did not escape death. And then Enoch is the exception since it was stated, "He did not see death." Here's a similar example to help illustrate.

> Back in my day we couldn't get to the stadium without taking the bus. We all lived so far away. Enoch though, had a car, so he could drive himself and didn't have to take the bus.
>
> However, Noah lived about 10 miles south of the stadium and so he rode the 17 bus to get there.
>
> Abraham, lived about 12 miles east of the stadium in a bad neighborhood that was not his own, and he shared a house with Isaac and Jacob. They had to take the 13 bus.
>
> Sarah lived about 20 miles north of the stadium and actually had to take the train downtown and then take the 15 bus.
>
> These all took buses because they didn't live near the stadium, but seeing how they could get there by bus, they gladly did. Especially since they loved going to all the football games.

Conclusion

It is impossible to claim there is a legitimate contradiction here because grammatically there isn't one. But since so many oppose God and His Word, they will look for contradictions — even if they must twist logic and rules of grammar to find them.

Can God Be Tempted?

← Chris Russell →

The Bible clearly states that God cannot be tempted by evil, so why do other passages speak of God being tempted?

The "Problem"

Some have imagined a contradiction in the Scriptures regarding whether or not God can be tempted. These readers are confused when they compare passages such as the following:

> Let no one say when he is tempted, "I am tempted by God"; for God cannot be tempted by evil, nor does He Himself tempt anyone (James 1:13).

> Therefore the people contended with Moses, and said, "Give us water, that we may drink." So Moses said to them, "Why do you contend with me? Why do you tempt the LORD?" (Exodus 17:2).

Since one passage states that God cannot be tempted and the other claims that God was tempted, how can Christians avoid a contradiction here?

The Solution

We should also consider Deuteronomy 6:16, which instructs the Israelites to be careful that they do not to tempt the Lord. Likewise, Malachi 3:15 refers to the wicked who tempt God with their evil lifestyles. Jesus even quoted the Old Testament Scriptures when He warned others not to tempt the Lord (e.g., Matthew 4:7 and Luke 4:12).

Today, we mostly use the term *tempt* specifically to mean to "solicit to do evil." However, the term has not always been quite so narrowly interpreted. In the Bible this word conveys that idea at times, but at other times it means to "put to the test." The context helps to determine which meaning is intended.

James clearly stated, "God cannot be tempted *by evil*" (emphasis added). The phrase "by evil" is important because it highlights the point James was trying to make. This clearly indicates that God cannot be enticed to commit evil.

In the other passages above that referred to tempting God, the writers were using the term to mean we must not put God to the test. Here is the line of reasoning:

1. God has said He will judge sin.

2. When we sin, we are putting God to the test to see if He will respond to our sin by doing what He has said He will do.

3. We must not "test" the extent of God's grace but instead obey what He has told us to do.

Now, along with this question of whether or not God can be tempted, another potential dilemma arises, which is often stated like this:

1. James 1:13 tells us God cannot be tempted by evil.

2. According to Luke 4, Matthew 4, and Hebrews 4:15, Jesus was tempted by evil.

3. Therefore, Jesus was not God or this is a contradiction.

Off the cuff, Jesus was tempted by Satan, not evil. We need to keep in mind that Satan and evil are different. Though Satan is exceedingly evil, he cannot be interchanged with the term.

Furthermore, there are two keys to understanding this mystery. First, we must keep in mind the hypostatic union of the two natures of Christ. That's a pretty fancy way of saying that Jesus was fully man and fully God at the same time. Jesus had a fully human nature (but sinless), and He had the nature of God.

Second, it is important to understand the difference between internal enticement and external enticement. When Jesus was tempted, His temptation came from an external source: Satan (Luke

4:2; Matthew 4:1). When we are tempted, this comes right from within our own hearts due to our own sinful natures, although the temptation to sin can be kindled by something external. James 1:14 tells us, "But each one is tempted when he is drawn away by his own desires and enticed."

So could Jesus sin or not? This question has been debated by theologians for centuries, and although all true Christians agree that Jesus did not sin, they do not agree on whether or not He could have sinned. Other than agreeing that Jesus did not sin, *Answers in Genesis* does not hold a position on this debate. We would urge you to carefully and prayerfully study Scripture and consult with your local church on this subject.

There are three common views on the subject. Some hold the impeccability position (Latin *non posse peccare*). This view states that Christ could not have sinned, and thus was not even tempted, during Satan's attempts at "temptations." Others hold the peccability view (*posse non peccare*), meaning that He *could* have sinned. A third position attempts to find middle ground and is based on Christ having both a human nature and divine nature. This view says that in His human nature, He could have sinned, but in His divine nature, He could not.

Conclusion

The Bible does not contradict itself on these points. While God cannot be tempted to do evil, we are commanded not to put the Lord to the test. When it comes to the person of Jesus Christ, this issue may be more complex because He also had a fully human nature, but still no contradiction.

Why Don't Christians Follow all the Old Testament Laws?

⤺ Bodie Hodge ⤻

Are Christians living contradictions because they don't follow all of the Old Testament laws?

The Problem

Have you ever heard the claim that Christians are walking contradictions because they don't follow all the Old Testament laws (e.g., offering sin offerings, Leviticus 5:5-6)? Consider the following verses and think about whether Christians obey these commands, and if they do not, why don't they?

> Nevertheless these you shall not eat . . . the swine, though it divides the hoof, having cloven hooves, yet does not chew the cud, is unclean to you (Leviticus 11:4, 7).

> You shall not wear a garment of different sorts, such as wool and linen mixed together (Deuteronomy 22:11).

Many Christians eat bacon or wear garments made of different materials (which was but one of many illicit mixtures that defile). So how can they possibly claim to believe the Bible and follow God?

The Solution

The answer is not as difficult as it may seem, and yet is overlooked by non-Christians, and even some Christians, who have not read or at least fail to understand some basic theology. Did rules ever change in the Bible? Of course they did. Let's look at one example.

From the beginning man was vegetarian (Genesis 1:30). The Bible lists a number of covenants after this and usually there were some associated rule changes at this time. When there was a new covenant with Noah, man was allowed to eat clean and unclean meat (Genesis 9:3). With Moses, meat eating was even more strict, limiting them to eat only meat that was clean (e.g., Leviticus 11:47). In the new covenant in Christ's blood, this was further opened up (Romans 14:1–4).[1] And in heaven, we will be vegetarian again to complete the cycle (there will be no death in heaven [Revelation 21:4], so no meat will be available).[2]

Food permitted to be eaten

Edenic	Vegetarian
Noahic	Vegetarian foods, clean and unclean meats
Mosaic	Vegetarian foods, clean meats
New Covenant in Christ	Vegetarian foods, clean and unclean meats
Heaven	Vegetarian

For instance, Christians recognize from the Bible that when a new covenant came about, certain rules changed, were modified, or affirmed. Some of these covenants are the original Edenic,[3] Noahic, and the new one in Christ's blood.

---

1. Some still preferred to utilize diets that exclude meat, even though it was permitted in Scripture. For example, Daniel, who lived under the Mosaic covenant, followed a vegetarian diet instead of eating the king's delicacies while in captivity, and this was not a sin. In the New Covenant, some who are weak eat only vegetables (Romans 14:2). Of course, there are those with health issues that avoid meat. This is not sinful, since the New Testament does not command every Christian to eat meat, but allows it. Further, this answers the verse mentioned previously in Leviticus 11:4, 7.

2. Some may argue that meat could still be eaten without death, e.g., lizard tails can be removed and regrown without the death of an animal. If such could be designed to have no pain in heaven, this could theoretically allow meat to be eaten in a perfect heavenly state. Though, would such a thing be necessary in a perfect state? Likely not.

3. "But like men they transgressed the covenant; There they dealt treacherously with Me." (Hosea 6:7). Covenants are an agreement in a post-Fall world where things are no longer perfect and agreements need to be made between parties. Some theologians make distinctions between what have been called the Edenic covenant, the Adamic covenant, and the covenant of works. For the purposes of this example, we have chosen to utilize the

So God's rules *to man* can change at various covenants (but God's character has never changed). With regards to various laws, there are also some changes, but it may not be as "cut and dried" as the example above regarding food.

Two Major Schools of Thought

Now here is the tricky part: developing a theological basis *from the Bible* on the subject regarding law changes. Let's look from a bird's-eye view at the change from the Mosaic to New Covenant. From a big picture, there are two popular theological schools of thought (with many variations). They are *dispensational* and *covenant* theology.[4] These views have similarities and differences. They differ in the way they look at *how* the laws change. There is more to it than this, but we will get to that in a moment:

> **Covenant Theology:** *rules apply unless done away with in the next covenant.* In other words, each covenant is seen as part of a greater covenant that now has modifications where the rules are still in effect unless abrogated or modified ultimately by the New Testament by God.[5]

---

term "Edenic," but this should not be seen as an endorsement of a particular theological position.

4. In rare cases, some other Christians hold to views different from these two, but to answer this alleged contradiction I am going to stick to the main two theologies that Christians adhere to. So please forgive me if I have not dived into one of the other theological positions.

5. Leading Covenant Theologian Greg Bahnsen stated: "The methodological point, then, is that we presume our obligation to obey any Old Testament commandment unless the New Testament indicates otherwise. We must assume continuity with the Old Testament rather than discontinuity. This is not to say that there are no changes from Old to New Testament. Indeed, there are — important ones. However, the word of God must be the standard which defines precisely what those changes are for us; we cannot take it upon ourselves to assume such changes or read them into the New Testament. God's Word, His direction to us, must be taken as continuing in its authority until God Himself reveals otherwise. This is, in a sense, the heart of "covenant theology" over against a dispensational understanding of the relation between Old and New Testaments." Greg L. Bahnsen, *By This Standard: The Authority of God's Law Today* (Tyler, TX: Institute for Christian Economics, second printing, 1991), p. 3.

Dispensational Theology: *previous rules tend to be done away with in the New Covenant unless reiterated in that covenant.* In other words, the New Dispensation generally does away with previous Mosaic rules because those rules were given to a specific group of people, and new rules need to be stated.[6]

Both of these schools of thought affect the way Old Testament laws are viewed. Both sides agree on many laws because so much was reiterated, changed, or commented on in the New Testament.[7] But some things went away, such as the sacrificial stuff in Leviticus 5:5–6, which Christ fulfilled. Both of these schools of thought answer why Christians do not adhere to all the Mosaic laws.

There are Christians whose theologies do not fit into either of these camps or are variations of them. For example, within Dispensationalism there is (among others) Classic Dispensationalism, Revised Dispensational, Progressive Dispensationalism, and one theologian even used the term "Leaky" Dispensationalism.

On the other side of the coin, there is New Covenant Theology which finds some middle ground between Dispensationalism and Covenant Theology, but starts with a Covenant Theology basis as opposed to Dispensational basis.

This short response keeps me from going into the details of each position and their nuances. Furthermore, Answers in Genesis does

---

6. Leading Dispensationalist Charles Ryrie states: "Now the Mosaic Law was done away in its entirety as a code. It has been replaced by the law of Christ. The law of Christ contains some new commands (1 Tim. 4:4), some old ones (Rom. 13:9), and some revised ones (Rom. 13:4, with reference to capital punishment). All of the laws of the Mosaic code have been abolished because the code has. Specific Mosaic commands which are part of the Christian code appear there not as a continuation of part of the Mosaic Law, or in order to be observed in some deeper sense but as specifically incorporated into that code, and as such they are binding on believers today. A particular law that was part of the Mosaic code is done away; that same law, if part of the law of Christ, is binding." Charles C. Ryrie, *Basic Theology* (Colorado Springs, CO: ChariotVictor Publishing, 1982), p. 305.

7. Where they disagree is where it gets interesting. . . .

not take a position on this theological debate.[8] We encourage people to know what they believe on this debate as the authors and editors know where they stand on this issue, but have refrained from giving those positions favor in this response.

From here, we let your denomination go further. So if you are interested in pursuing these theologies in more detail, then I suggest you contact your local pastor and elders and do further research to get into the finer details. This is all said to teach the reader that Christians have a *biblical basis* for certain law changes and can easily answer the claim that Christians are walking contradictions.

---

8. Answers in Genesis (AiG) is a unique ministry for this time — a biblical authority ministry. AiG is a *parachurch* ministry staffed by church members from various denominations (e.g., Baptist, Evangelical Free, Christian, Lutheran, Presbyterian, etc.) to focus on specific issues and challenges of today's culture surrounding biblical authority. So internal theological debates are not the focus here at the ministry, so long as the debaters use the Bible as *authoritative* in the debate, which seems to be the case with this issue. Please do not get us wrong, this is an important debate, but we will let others lead the fight on this one. For more on our biblical authority stance please see: "Where Do We Draw the Line?" Bodie Hodge, AiG website: http://www.answersingenesis.org/articles/2009/10/19/where-do-we-draw-the-line.

Conclusion
← Tim Chaffey (with Bodie Hodge) →

It is privilege to be a part of *Answers in Genesis*, a ministry that upholds the authority of God's Word from the first verse to the last. But all Christians should be involved in defending the truth of Scripture through words and deeds. If we claim to follow Christ, then how can we reject parts of the Bible (Christ's Word) either through outright denial of clear biblical teachings (i.e., young earth, worldwide Flood, etc.) or through a lifestyle that denies its authority over our lives?

This book has been designed to show you that we can trust the entire Bible. By tackling over 40 supposed contradictions from various sections of Scripture, we have once again demonstrated that the Bible can withstand assaults from the critics and skeptics alike.

This work has also shown that a person does not need to be a scholar to answer these types of objections. Every Christian is capable of adequately handling these issues. This book series has been written by people with all levels of education — from those with PhDs to a youngster in middle school! So we hope this is an encouragement to help you realize that we can all do our part to answer the false claims of contradictions in the Bible.

To further assist you in this area, please consider the following principles when dealing with an alleged contradiction.

First, remember that you will not understand every portion of Scripture. Since God's ways are higher than man's ways (Isaiah 55:8–9), and since the secret things belong to the Lord (Deuteronomy 29:29), we need to realize that we won't be able to figure out everything.

Second, just because something is hard to understand or accept does not mean it is false. We all struggle to some degree to grasp the concept of the Trinity (God is one being in three persons). That makes sense, since God is infinite and we are finite. However, some people have rejected this doctrine and accuse those who believe it of heresy. In reality, the foundational teachings of this doctrine are clearly laid out in Scripture[1] and we need to humbly accept it — even if we cannot fully comprehend the triune nature of God. Furthermore, we would be worried if a fallible, sinful, finite person really thought they could comprehend an infinite God!

Third, remember that the original manuscripts were inspired by God. What we have today are translations of copies of those originals. So when we come across a difficulty, we need to see if there was an error made by the translators, or if there may have been a copyist error. By comparing Scripture with Scripture, and checking various translations along with the Hebrew and Greek texts and copies, it is usually fairly easy to make these determinations.

Fourth, context, context, context! If you have read each of the chapters in this book, then you know how important it is to examine the context of every relevant passage. Most of the problems can be quickly resolved by studying the passage in its entirety and paying close attention to what it *does* and *does not* state.

Fifth, these alleged contradictions often disappear through careful and prayerful study. Ask the Lord to guide you in your study of His Word. Rely on His wisdom and have a teachable spirit.

Sixth, as we discussed in the introduction, sometimes we need to go on the offensive. We can easily demonstrate the irrational nature of other belief systems in the world, and only biblical Christianity offers a rational, coherent, and consistent foundation for knowledge, laws of logic, and morality. For example, when a skeptic claims the Bible is guilty of breaking a law of logic, point out how "their worldview has no basis for logic to even exist, and that it is very Christian of the unbeliever to think it does." So he must assume the Bible is true just to argue against it.[2]

---

1. http://www.answersingenesis.org/articles/2008/02/20/god-is-triune.

2. For more on this see: Dr. Jason Lisle, *The Ultimate Proof of Creation* (Green Forest, AR: Master Books, 2009).

Finally, have complete confidence in the Author. Since God is the ultimate Author of Scripture, then we can be sure that He will not contradict Himself (2 Timothy 2:13). Keep in mind that the handful of supposed contradictions (and these can easily be answered) pales in comparison to the number of biblical facts that have been confirmed via other sources. The Bible has demonstrated its trustworthiness in so many ways. For example, hundreds of detailed prophecies have been fulfilled perfectly, and thousands of archaeological sites have been found precisely where the Bible described them. Skeptics used to question the existence of many of these places, yet after more "digging" the Bible was shown to be accurate. Similarly, through more digging into the Word, solutions can be found to the supposed contradictions.

It is often helpful to cross-examine your own beliefs. For example, try to "disprove" the Resurrection, and you'll quickly see how poor the alternative ideas truly are. God's Word will pass every test.

I (Bodie Hodge) was on a bus in Peru speaking to a pastor from that country. When the pastor found out that I worked in an apologetics ministry, he raised one of the supposed contradictions covered in this book regarding the livestock in Egypt. Now, this man was not attacking Scripture as many critics do. He loved God and His Word, but he had really struggled with this issue for years, without an answer. He was thrilled when we opened the Bible and read the passage in context and I gave him an answer that reduced the alleged contradiction to ashes. He was so excited! He knew there was a solution, but he just needed a little help in getting the answer. And sometimes we are all like that.

This story illustrates the proper attitude a person needs to have when confronted with these difficulties. He had complete confidence in the Author. This man still trusted God, even though he struggled to reconcile the passages in Scripture. Sadly, too many people fail to dig deeper to find an answer, or worse, they close their Bible and allow their doubts to lead to unbelief.

May we always have complete confidence in God and His Word and rely on Him for all things. "It is better to trust in the LORD than to put confidence in man" (Psalm 118:8).

A Library of Answers
for Families and Churches

Over 100 faith-affirming answers to some of the
most-questioned topics about faith, science, & the Bible.

Also
available
in digital
format.

$55.99 | 978-0-89051-819-9

To help you find the answers, **Ken Ham** and the team of apologetic experts at
Answers in Genesis authored *The New Answers Book Volumes 1, 2, 3,* and *4*. This
top-selling series is now available as a complete collection. Prepare yourself, your
family, and your church to answer the questions of friends, and skeptics, and
defend against the prevalent secular humanist culture that is invading our schools,
government, and even the Christian community with this four-book set.

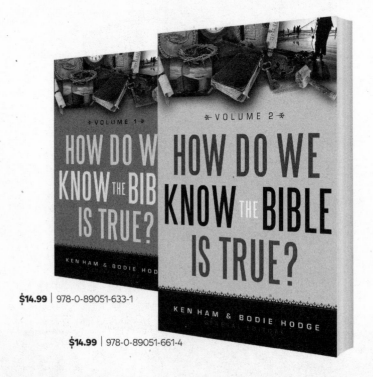

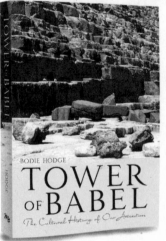